KU-672-947

GAIL DEIBLER FINKE

creative edge

BROCHURES

HBI

COPYRIGHT

Creative Edge: Brochures.
First published 2000 by North Light Books.

Distributed outside the United States and Canada by
HarperCollins International
10 East 53rd Street
New York, NY 10022-5299
Fax: 212-207-7654

 Published by North Light Books, an imprint of F&W Publications, Inc., 1507 Dana Avenue, Cincinnati, Ohio 45207. (800) 289-0963. First edition.

04 03 02 01 00   5 4 3 2 1

Library of Congress Cataloging-in-Publication Data

Finke, Gail, 1964-
Creative edge—brochures / Gail Deibler Finke.— 1st ed.
p. cm.
Includes indexes.
ISBN 0-06-019886-9 (alk. paper)
1. Pamphlets—Design. 2. Pamphlets—United States—Design. I. Title: Brochures. II. Title.
Z246 .F56 2000
686.2'252—dc21   99-044082
CIP

Editor: Linda H. Hwang
Production Coordinator: Kristen Heller
Interior Designer: Stephanie Strang
Production Artist: Tari Sasser
Photographers: Al Parrish, Christine Polomsky

dedication

THANKS to all the designers whose inspiring work gives North Light Books something to print, and me something to write about. THANKS to the North Light art department, who transform piles of paper and transparencies into things of beauty. THANKS to the photographers and printers, who make the photos look almost as good as the real thing. THANKS to my editors, who let me do this work. **And THANKS to my family,** who give me the reason to do it. Meghan and Marshal, this book is for you.

TABLE

table of [contents]

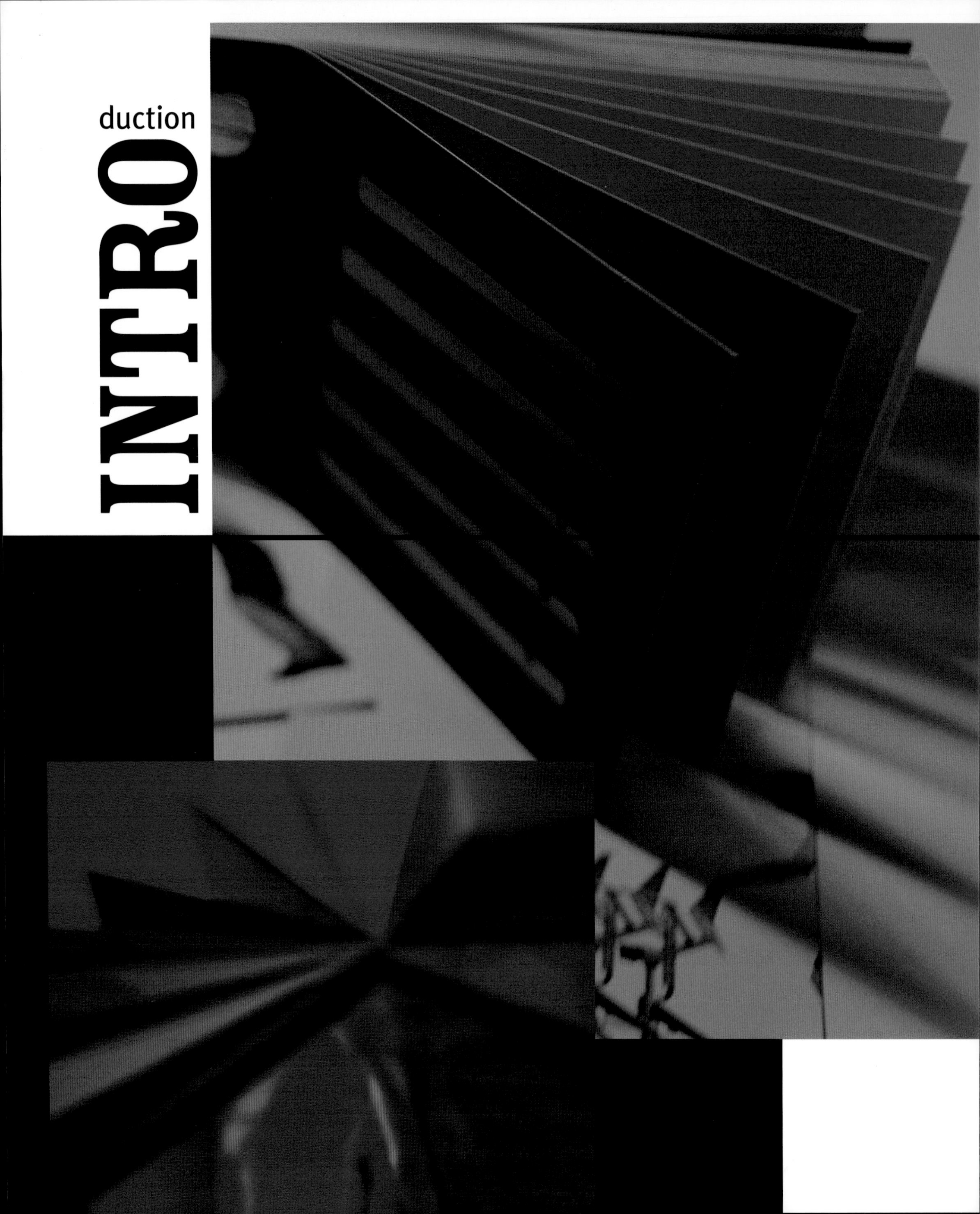
INTRO
duction

Brochures.

The term conjures up images of, well, boredom. Folded sheets of paper crammed with color photographs—smiling people, picturesque landmarks, new products. Something you pick up at an airport or hotel, a convention or store. Something that comes in the mail, in a fat and unsolicited envelope, briefly raising hopes for a more interesting day but (usually) dashing them.

You won't find anything like that here. In fact, anyone lucky enough to receive one of the brochures featured on these pages would be guaranteed at least a few minutes without boredom. The pieces here were designed to engage, enrage, delight and affright. Some will make you laugh (try p. 111 and p. 152 for more than a few chuckles). Some can make you cry. I cried when I read the Andy Post Flashlight book (page 142). And I don't think it's just me.

The designers featured here have accomplished the remarkable. They've all gone beyond simple words and images, combining them in a way that's fresh and bold. You'll find work from throughout the United States and around the world, work of every description and style. What unites these 120 pieces is their unexpected punch, their ***creative edge***.

If you manage to design a brochure without using any type, let us know. You might be able to get away with it on a poster, but by definition a brochure has to let the user know what he or she is looking at, and why.

That said, there's no reason that brochure type has to be dull. Even the most staid businesses and products can benefit from the many exciting type options now available to designers. From computer manipulation to old-fashioned pen and paper, type has never been so versatile.

[type]

[type] I

in this section, you'll see how:

- Gee + Chung used letters and lines to transform a client's name into networking diagrams.
- Designer/typographer Fritz Klaetke used letterpress printing, a dot pattern and his own typeface to unify a portfolio of his firm's diverse work.
- Paul Nicholson designed sets of letters (rather than complete alphabets) and included text in numerous languages with non-Western letterforms to illustrate his firm's versatility.

TYPORNOGRAPHY
adult adventures in typographic treatment
i iS A BiG HiT WiTH ALL THE LADiES
Y taking up the rear in orgy

STUDIO: Creative Activity Design Company, Toronto, Ontario, Canada **ART DIRECTOR/DESIGNER:** Matthew Beckerle **ILLUSTRATOR:** Matthew Beckerle **PHOTOGRAPHER:** Matthew Beckerle **CLIENT:** Self **SOFTWARE:** QuarkXPress, Adobe Illustrator, Adobe Photoshop **PAPER:** Gloss Text **COLORS:** 4, process **PAGES:** 24 **SIZE:** 3¾" x 3¾" (9.5cm x 9.5cm) **PRINT RUN:** 300 **COST PER UNIT:** US$3 **TYPEFACES:** ITC Cooper Black, DIN Schriften, DIN, OCR-B, Officina Serif **INSPIRATION:** "A play on words," says designer Matthew Beckerle. "It was a chance to take a taboo subject and create something savvy, sophisticated and fun, without offending others." **CONCEPT:** "Type was used to illustrate the mood or idea, through individual shape, placement or phonetics. Each spread expressed one vowel within one word. Every word could suggest a sexual connotation, depending on how you look at it." **SPECIAL FOLDS OR FEATURES:** Center gatefold. **SPECIAL COST-CUTTING TECHNIQUES:** "All pieces were cut and assembled by hand."

STUDIO: Epigram Pte Ltd., Singapore **ART DIRECTOR:** Paul van der Veer **DESIGNERS:** Paul van der Veer, Andrew Dallas Naylor, Lee Huei Peng **ILLUSTRATOR:** Andrew Dallas Naylor **PHOTOGRAPHER:** Beh Kay Yi (artists' portrait) **CLIENT/SERVICE:** A Ton of Bricks/art gallery **SOFTWARE:** QuarkXPress **PAPER:** Book Design (cover); Saltine Textured (text); Exel Matt (photos) **COLORS:** 4, process plus fluorescent pink and spot varnish **PAGES:** 4-page cover; 50-page text **SIZE:** 7½" x 8⅝" (19cm x 22cm) **PRINT RUN:** 1,000 **TYPEFACES:** Various **CONCEPT:** This catalog for an art exhibit by three graphic designers was inspired by the exhibit's name, Peep Show. Die-cut circles in the cover reveal three eyes, the eyes of the designers. Their work, in turn, reveals truths about Singapore, where one was born and the others chose to live and work. **SPECIAL FEATURES:** Rivet binding. **SPECIAL COST-CUTTING TECHNIQUES:** Text and cover were printed in one color on textured, uncoated paper. Photos were printed on glossy stock; spot varnish gives them even greater definition.

STUDIO: The Designers Republic, Sheffield, U.K. **ART DIRECTOR:** The Designers Republic **DESIGNER:** The Designers Republic **ILLUSTRATOR:** The Designers Republic **PHOTOGRAPHY:** Archive, stock, featured artists' own photography, The Designers Republic **CLIENT/SERVICE:** The Site Gallery, Sheffield, U.K./art gallery **SOFTWARE:** Macromedia FreeHand, Adobe Photoshop **COLORS:** Match metallic silver (cover); 4, process plus match metallic silver (interior) **PAGES:** 52 **SIZE:** 10⅞" x 7⅝" (27.5cm x 19.5cm) **PRINT RUN:** 1,000 **TYPEFACES:** Swiss 721 Condensed Italic, Swiss 721 Bold Condensed, OCR-A, OCR-B, Helvetica 55, Helvetica 75, Computerfont, DR Grumpface (DR Font), DR Store Lite (DR Font), DR TYP01 FG Squareular (DR Font); additional typefaces created by "Brain-Aided Design" **INSPIRATION:** Working with the designers whose work was featured in the exhibit, The Designers Republic says it was inspired by "the spirit of the computer-art pioneers of the Cybernetic Serendipity Exhibition and computer/digital art in general." **CONCEPT:** "Process/function. 'Star Dot Star' is programming language for 'everything.' The Star Dot Star exhibition revisited the aesthetics and concepts of the original Cybernetic Serendipity Exhibition held at The ICA (London) in 1968, the first major art exhibition dedicated to computer art." **SPECIAL PRODUCTION TECHNIQUES:** Embossed cover.

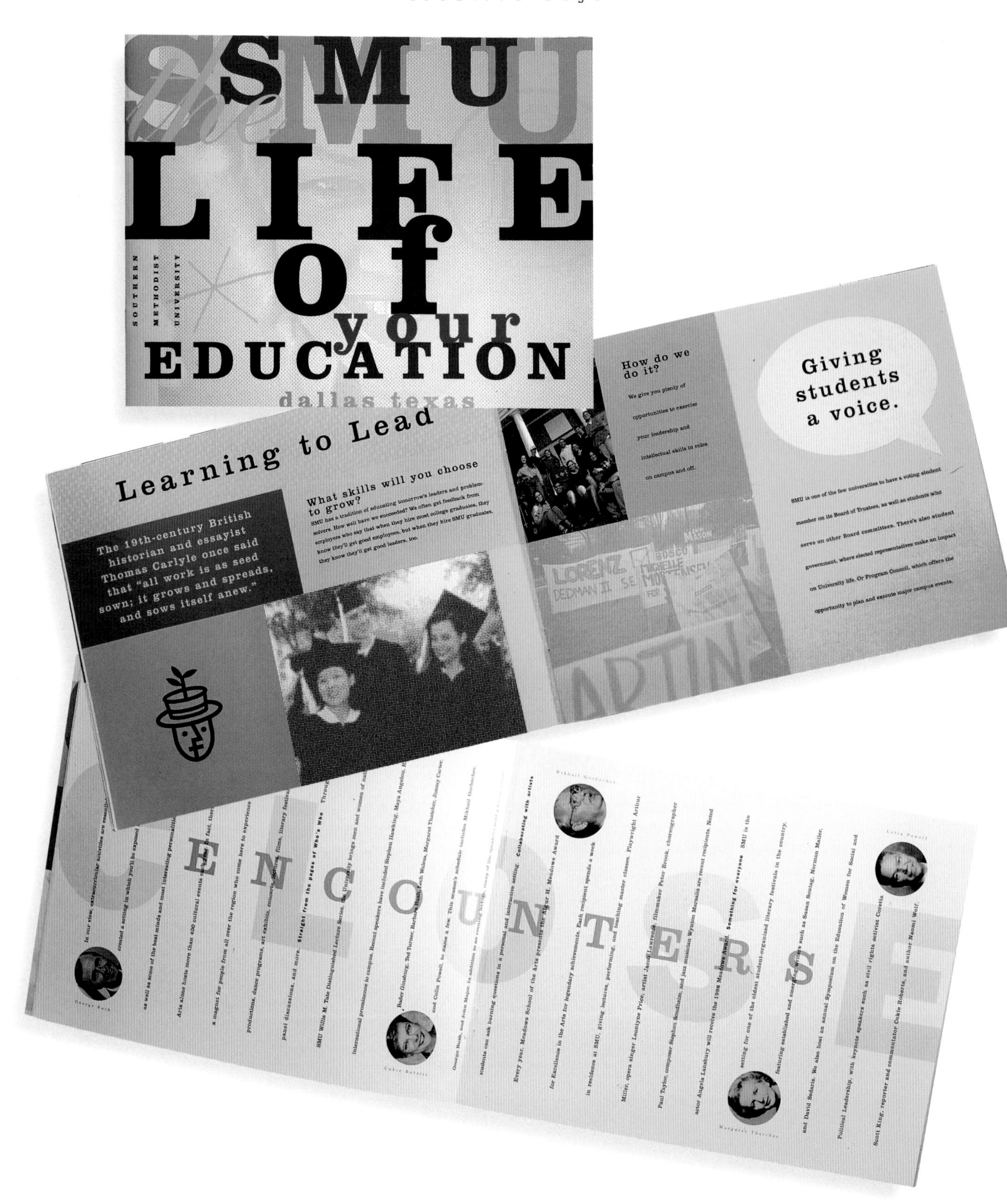

STUDIO: Brainstorm, Inc., Dallas, TX **ART DIRECTOR/STUDIO:** Chuck Johnson/Brainstorm, Inc.; Vicki Olvera/SMU Publications **DESIGNER:** Chuck Johnson **ILLUSTRATORS:** Chuck Johnson, Tom Kirsch **PHOTOGRAPHER:** Hillsman Jackson **CLIENT:** Southern Methodist University **SOFTWARE:** QuarkXPress, Adobe Illustrator, Adobe Photoshop **COLORS:** 4, process plus 1, match and varnish **PAGES:** 32 plus cover **SIZE:** 8½" x 11" (21.6cm x 27.9cm) **TYPEFACES:** Adobe Garamond, Franklin Gothic, Clarendon **INSPIRATION:** "The contrast of a beautiful campus and classical architecture with students with cutoffs, tattoos and body piercing," says designer Chuck Johnson. **CONCEPT:** "The purpose of this brochure is to entice high school students to apply to Southern Methodist University. The book is divided into two sections, and is basically two brochures that meet in the center at a big gatefold. One half is the academic side of college life, titled 'The Education of Your Life.' This section has a classic, traditional design approach with a lot of text. Flip the book over, and the second half (titled 'The Life of Your Education') focuses on the lifestyle and life learning experiences that students get at college. It has a fun, modern design approach, with oversize type and bite-sized bits of information." **SPECIAL FEATURES:** The piece has two "front covers" and a large, central horizontal gatefold. It was mailed in a vellum envelope. **SPECIAL COST-CUTTING TECHNIQUES:** "Many photos were from SMU's vast library of photography."

STUDIO: Pentagram Design, New York, NY **ART DIRECTOR:** Michael Bierut **DESIGNERS:** Michael Bierut, Jacqueline Thaw **PRINTER:** Lithographix Inc., Los Angeles **CLIENT/SERVICE:** Mohawk Paper Mills, Inc./paper manufacturer **SOFTWARE:** Adobe Photoshop, Adobe Illustrator, QuarkXPress **PAPER:** Mohawk Ultrafelt Cover Black (cover); Mohawk Superfine Text Ultrawhite Smooth (pp. 1–12); Mohawk 50/1 Plus Text Bright White (pp. 14–24); Mohawk Options Text Bright White Smooth (pp. 25–48); Mohawk Superfine Text White Eggshell (pp. 49–60) **COLORS:** Matte foil and tinted gloss varnish (cover); 4, process plus various varnishes, match colors, and UV inks (interiors) **PAGES:** 60 **SIZE:** 10½" x 9¾" (26.7cm x 24.8cm) **TYPEFACES:** Mrs. Eaves (Zuzana Licko); Trade Gothic (Jackson Burke); Trade Stencil (Michael Johnson) **CONCEPT:** "This is the fourth installment of *Rethinking Design*, a series published by Mohawk Paper Mills to explore issues of interest to designers," says Pentagram. "Guest editor Janet Abrams was invited to devise a theme that could be timed to the AIGA Conference in New Orleans. Her idea was to explore the varied definitions of the word 'medium': medium as a channel of communication, as average, as in-between, as transmitter of messages from the spirit world. A variety of writers, photographers and designers were invited to help bring these different meanings to life, to make a paper promotion that designers wouldn't throw away after a minute or two." **SPECIAL PRODUCTION TECHNIQUES:** The word "medium" is die-cut into the cover. Beneath it, on a limited edition of the books, the word was airbrushed by hand. Various spot and overall varnishes, UV inks and other printing effects throughout the book emphasize the artwork and fine printing, showing the paper's qualities.

?
Etec
on
Technology
We have to be different to show others the way.
who?

STUDIO: Cahan & Associates, San Francisco, CA **ART DIRECTOR:** Bill Cahan **DESIGNER:** Lian Ng **ILLUSTRATOR:** Roxanna Bikadoroff **CLIENT/SERVICE:** Etec Systems/high tech, pattern generation **SOFTWARE:** QuarkXPress **PAPER:** Mead Signature Silk **COLORS:** 6 over 6, match **PAGES:** 48 pages plus cover **SIZE:** 6⅝" x 4¾" (16.8cm x 12cm) **TYPEFACES:** Minion, Trade Gothic Condensed **CONCEPT:** "An introduction to who Etec is," says designer Lian Ng. Large words printed on two-page spreads ask the prospective employee's questions (who? why?). Naive artwork and blocks of friendly type answer them. Larger type on colored pages gives quick, "big picture" answers, while smaller type on white pages gives details. The bright colors and cheerful art give the high-tech company an inviting human face. **SPECIAL PRODUCTION TECHNIQUES:** Hand-bound cover. **SPECIAL COST-CUTTING TECHNIQUES:** The book's small size meant that all pages could be printed on one sheet.

Overview of 1998

[illegible]

Results of Operations

[illegible]

This is what we do Etec Systems, Inc. designs, manufactures and markets patterning solutions that enable the production of the faster, smaller and cheaper semiconductor chips and printed circuit boards necessary for today's electronics. With over 70% worldwide market share for semiconductor IC mask pattern generation (PG) equipment — equipment that makes semiconductor masks — Etec is widely recognized for its expertise with laser- and electron-beam PG technologies. Today, Etec is also leveraging semiconductor solutions into the printed circuit board (PCB) industry with revolutionary laser direct imaging technology.

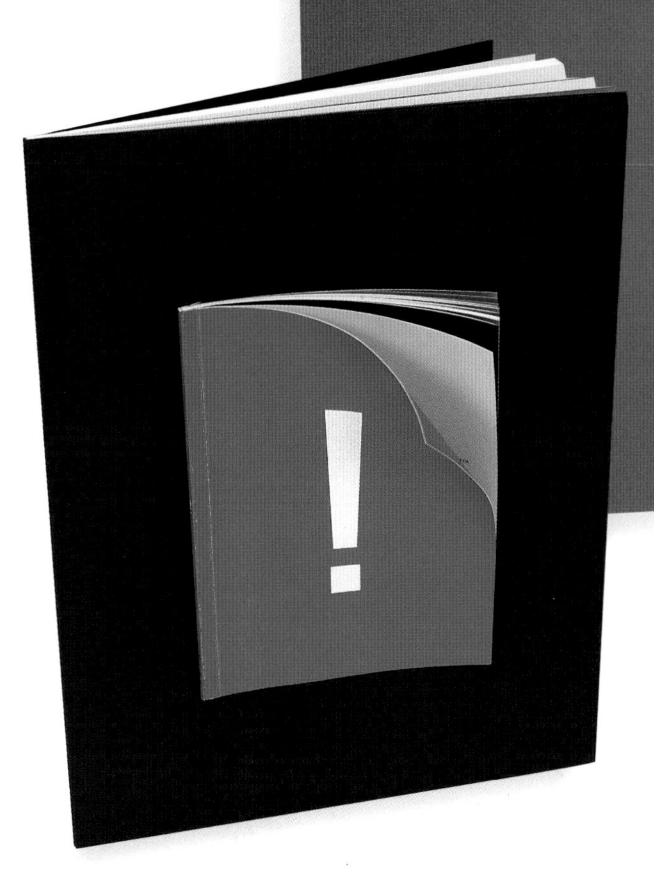

STUDIO: Cahan & Associates, San Francisco, CA **ART DIRECTOR:** Bill Cahan **DESIGNER:** Lian Ng **PHOTOGRAPHERS:** various **CLIENT/SERVICE:** Etec Systems/high tech, pattern generation **SOFTWARE:** QuarkXPress **PAPER:** S.D. Warren Patina, Fox River Cover (cover of big book), Weyerhaeuser Cougar (big book), Mead Signature (small book) **COLORS:** 6 over 6, match plus metallic (small book); 4 over 4, match (big book) **PAGES:** 52 (small book); 42 (big book) **SIZE:** 6½" x 4¾" (16.5cm x 12cm) (small book); 11½" x 9" (29.2cm x 22.9cm) (big book) **TYPEFACES:** Bembo, Trade Gothic **INSPIRATION:** "The recruitment book, which is a small hand-bound book introducing Etec," says designer Lian Ng. **CONCEPT:** "A two-in-one piece that acts as both an annual report and a product brochure. The product brochure also acts as a follow-up piece to the recruitment brochure." The small product brochure features playful type, bright colors, and clean but friendly design. The annual report, printed largely in metallic ink, has a more formal, corporate look. **SPECIAL FEATURES:** A pocket slit on the cover of the big book holds the little book in place.

STUDIO: Murphy Design Inc., Cleveland, OH **DESIGNER:** Mark Murphy **ILLUSTRATOR:** Mark Murphy **PHOTOGRAPHERS:** various performance artists **CLIENT/SERVICE:** Cleveland Performance Art Festival/nonprofit foundation promoting performance art **SOFTWARE:** QuarkXPress, Macromedia FreeHand **PAPER:** French Butcher White **COLORS:** 1, match plus black **PAGES:** 32 **SIZE:** 8" x 5½" (20.3cm x 14cm) **PRINT RUN:** 20,000 **COST PER UNIT:** US$1.35 **TYPEFACES:** Futura, Modula, Clique Wedge, typewriter, Garamond **INSPIRATION:** "I wanted the layouts to tell a story about each performance," says designer Mark Murphy. **CONCEPT:** Using only two colors, Murphy wanted to "inspire performance artist fans and the general public to attend various events over a three-month performance calendar. The piece needed to make a lot of information seem light." **SPECIAL COST-CUTTING TECHNIQUES:** The size of the brochure was determined by the maximum printable area on a single press sheet.

STUDIO: Visual Dialogue, Boston, MA **ART DIRECTOR:** Fritz Klaetke **DESIGNERS:** Fritz Klaetke, Carol Hayes **PHOTOGRAPHER:** Kent Dayton **CLIENT:** Self **SOFTWARE:** Adobe Photoshop, QuarkXPress **PAPER:** Fox River Starwhite Vicksburg **COLORS:** Letterpress gold (cover); 4, process (recto pages), letterpress gold (verso pages) (interior) **PAGES:** 9 plus cover **SIZE:** $3\frac{3}{4}$" x $5\frac{7}{8}$" (9.5cm x 15cm) **PRINT RUN:** 250 **COST PER UNIT:** approx. US$25 **TYPEFACES:** News Halftone (cover and back) (Fritz Klaetke); News Gothic (captions). "News Gothic was converted to a grayscale tint of black in Photoshop," says designer Fritz Klaetke, "then converted to bitmap mode with a coarse dot screen—hence, 'News Halftone.'" **CONCEPT:** "In tackling what has to be the hardest project for a design—one's own self-promo—the objective was to target potential clients who are smart and appreciate the importance of design. To this end, we combined a statement of the studio's design objectives, which runs through the brochure, with portfolio sample cards, which can be re-combined in many ways." **SPECIAL PRODUCTION TECHNIQUES:** Letterpress, embossing and die-cutting. **SPECIAL COST-CUTTING TECHNIQUES:** Custom assembly (hand stapling).

Życie jest piękne - Lust och fägring stor
scen. i reż.: Bo Widerberg,
zdj.: Martin Bruus,
muz.: Georg Friedrich Haendel,
wyst.: Johan Widerberg (Stig Santesson), Marika Lagercrantz (Viola Jensson Gruter), Tomas von Brömssen (Kjell "Frank" Jensson), Nina Gunke (Stina Santesson),
Niemcy, 1995 r., 130 min.

"Życie jest piękne" oparte jest na spojrzeniach, nimi żyje. Pod dialogami kryje się, dużo od nich ważniejsza, gra spojrzeń.

Bo Widerberg

Miłość może narodzić się w najbardziej nieoczekiwanych okolicznościach, nawet między 37-letnią nauczycielką i 14-letnim uczniem.(...) Kontakt erotyczny między nauczycielką a uczniem (lub nauczycielem a uczennicą) jest jedynym tabu
z ostatnich) naszej cywilizacji, trochę jak
że o tym wie przede wszystkim nauczycielka.
wie także, ale jest młody, łamie zasady- i
nimi góruje. Czuje się zwycięzcą. To

Interesowała mnie ekstremalność tej
miałem świadomość, że nie jest to coś
mnie równie ważne jak sam temat inicjacji,
za sprawą jego doświadczeń ze światem dorosłych.
z o wiele starszą kobietą był więc ważny,
na znaczeniu.

Stig poznaje męża nauczycielki, widuje go
Rodzi się między nimi przyjaźń, może koleżeństwo.
głębsze więzy zaczynają łączyć Stiga ze zdradzonym
kochanką. Wiele osób mówiło mi, że ten zwrot akcji
ogromną niespodzianką. Okazywało się, że mężczyzna
więcej do dania chłopcu niż kobieta.(...)

Chłopak widzi, że mężczyzna jest zupełnie bezradny wobec swej żony - i to z kolei budzi w nim współczucie. Efekt jest taki, że chłopak czuje się coraz gorzej w sytuacji, w której się znalazł. Buntuje się, okazuje agresję swej kochance. Viola zaczyna bronić się przed jego buntem, widzi w nim zagrożenie.

Nauczycielka jest osobą niemoralną. Ale nie staramy się tego podkreślać nazbyt uporczywie. Film jest właściwie posępną i cyniczną komedią - mimo to miłość między Violą a Stigiem nie wygląda ani śmiesznie, ani brzydko czy wulgarnie. Niewiele tu scen erotycznych. Pierwsze zbliżenie między Violą a Stigiem odbywa się poza kadrem. Później jest scena miłosna na dywanie, ale chodzi w niej przede wszystkim o to, by pokazać jak Viola pięknieje. Pod wpływem swojej miłości otwiera się jak pąk kwiatu.

Kino szwedzkie przedstawiło już w innym znakomitym filmie gimnazjalistę, który znalazł się w takiej samej sytuacji potępienia i niesprawiedliwej kary za zakazaną miłość. To *Skandal* Sjöberga z roku 1944, według scenariusza młodego Ingmara Bergmana. Aluzja wydaje się oczywista. Jest w tym też rodzaj hołdu. Zarazem związek obu filmów wydaje się świetnie określać to, co tak drażniło Widerberga, gdy jeszcze jako publicysta ruszył przeciwko Bergmanowi w roku 1962.

Skandal to patetyczny i mroczny dramat; *Życie jest piękne* nazwał autor posępną i liryczną komedią. Filmy Bergmana zaludniają rozszarpujący się samotnicy wyizolowani z tła ogólnego; Widerberg ciepło pokazuje ludzkie więzi na tle tak precyzyjnie zarysowanym społecznie, jak precyzyjnie dobiera każde własnoręczne cięcie montażowe, a potem każdy detal - od kaczuszki przeciw
po prawdziwe superfortece B-17 wracające znad
ma miejsce w czasie II wojny
to uznać, umieszczając

STUDIO: Acrobat, Gdansk, Poland **ART DIRECTOR/DESIGNER:** Robert Bak **ILLUSTRATOR:** Robert Bak **CLIENT:** Baltic Culture Centre **SOFTWARE:** Macromedia FreeHand, Adobe Photoshop **PAPER:** Nopacoat Matte (cover); Lumiart (text) **COLORS:** 2, match **PAGES:** 40 **SIZE:** 8¼" x 8¼" (21cm x 21cm) **COST PER UNIT:** 5.00 pln (US$1.25) **TYPEFACE:** Rotis Semi Serif **CONCEPT:** "To connect the two different personalities of Swedish cinema in one publication," says designer Robert Bak.

STUDIO: Büro für Gestaltung, Offenbach, Germany **DESIGNERS:** Christoph Burkardt, Albrecht Hotz **PHOTOGRAPHER:** Betsy Green **CLIENT/SERVICE:** Drukkerij Rosbeek BV, The Netherlands/printer **SOFTWARE:** QuarkXPress **PAPER:** Art paper, Job Art mat **COLORS:** 4, process plus matte varnish **PAGES:** 112 **SIZE:** 7¾" x 7¾" (19.7cm x 19.7cm) **PRINT RUN:** 2,000 **TYPEFACES:** Joanna (body copy), Copperplate (headlines) **INSPIRATION:** "The photographs in this book show old borderstones around the region of Limburg in the heart of Europe. The texts deal with that theme on a more general and philosophic level," say designers Christoph Burkardt and Albrecht Hotz. "We tried to transform the structure and quality of these old stones to the cover, as described below. The graphic design of the pages is based on a systematic grid that is handled loosely. The same type and typesize are used throughout, but the positioning of pictures and type is arranged individually on every page. The numbers on the stones form separate typographical elements that substitute for page numbers, but are not placed in a continuous order. So different levels of perception that penetrate each other arise. There is a balance between the individual approach of each page and the overall effect, in which every viewer has to find his own place." **SPECIAL PRODUCTION TECHNIQUES:** "The cover is a specially selected cardboard that is silkscreen printed. The structure of the cardboard varies, so every copy is unique. All photographs are matte varnished to give them a dense and warm quality."

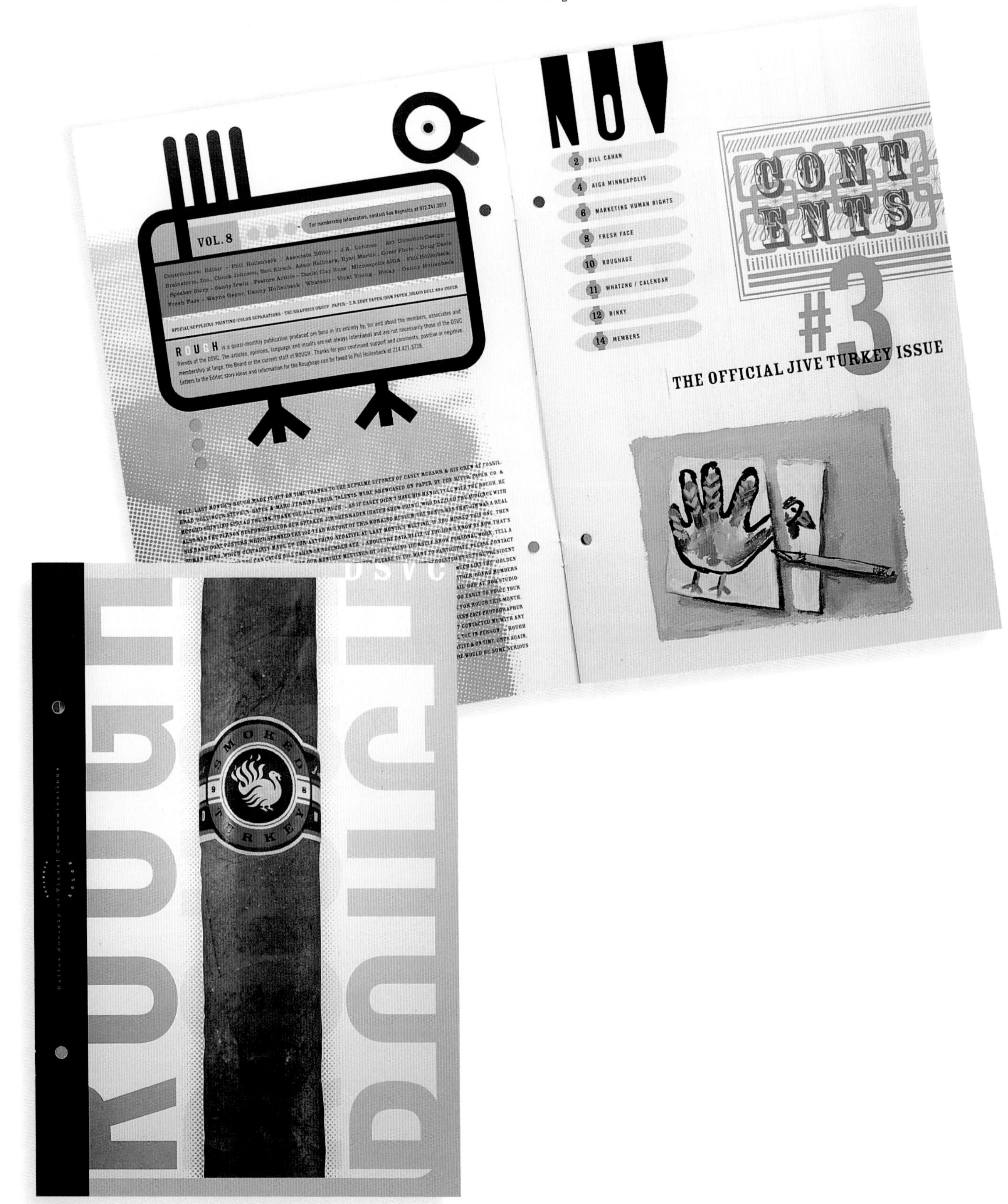

STUDIO: Brainstorm, Inc., Dallas, TX **ART DIRECTORS:** Chuck Johnson, Tom Kirsch, Adam Hallmark, Ryan Martin **DESIGNERS:** Chuck Johnson, Tom Kirsch, Adam Hallmark, Ryan Martin **ILLUSTRATORS:** Chuck Johnson, Tom Kirsch, Adam Hallmark, Ryan Martin **PHOTOGRAPHERS:** Doug Davis, Phil Hollenbeck, Danny Hollenbeck **EDITOR:** Phil Hollenbeck **CLIENT/ SERVICE:** Dallas Society of Visual Communications/advertising club **SOFTWARE:** QuarkXPress, Adobe Illustrator, Adobe Photoshop **PAPER:** E.B. Eddy Bravo Dull Cover **COLORS:** 4, process plus match metallic and tinted varnish **PAGES:** 12 plus cover **SIZE:** 13" x 9" (33cm x 22.9cm) **PRINT RUN:** 2,500 **TYPEFACES:** Rosewood, Clarendon, Trade Gothic, Garamond 3, Frutiger **INSPIRATION:** "Thanksgiving, current events and no boundaries," says designer Chuck Johnson. **CONCEPT:** "*Rough* is a monthly publication produced pro bono for members, associates and friends of the DSVC, one of the country's largest advertising clubs. This issue has a Thanksgiving/turkey theme. The satirical cigar cover was inspired by a political current event. *Rough* is a showcase for writing, design, photography and illustration. Individual spreads were divided among different designers with no standard format, to achieve a unique, fresh look." **SPECIAL PRODUCTION TECHNIQUES:** A silver tint varnish adds a new dimension to the artwork, which also featured metallic silver printing. **SPECIAL FOLDS OR FEATURES:** Ring punches add visual interest. **SPECIAL COST-CUTTING TECHNIQUES:** "The whole damn thing was produced for free."

First, I'd like to say that Dana Arnett hasn't paid me my hundred bucks.

HAPPY CAMPERS

ROUGHAGE

THE BODY SNATCHERS

I love Margie Bowles. She coined a term for AIGA. The body snatchers. And it suits that organization. Please don't get me wrong. I believe that AIGA is a viable organization that serves graphic designers much as ASMP serves photographers. Both organizations are well established & give their respective fields a national presence. But, in some cases, the market is large enough to support both a local club & a national chapter; i.e. the AIGA Dallas Chapter, the ASMP Dallas Chapter & the DSVC. The AIGA is presently wooing the DSVC to blend with the AIGA Dallas Chapter, but I can guarantee you it ain't gonna happen. Just as the clubs in Washington D.C. & Houston said no, so will we. Most cities of any size had their own clubs in the roaring eighties but, when the bust came, apathy set in & clubs folded. Enter AIGA, aka "Big Brother", & you now have AIGA Minneapolis, AIGA Austin, etc. All well & good for the pocketbook of AIGA National but what does that do for the designer at a local level? I can't answer that question but perhaps a call to Bryan Peterson would help. While I was in Minnesota at Design Camp, several people asked me if they could design a ROUGH. I explained that was not possible because it was a DSVC driven publication. Why not restart their local club & create their own "ROUGH"? Because then, as members of AIGA National, they would be supporting their industry and by establishing a local club, they could enjoy monthly functions, both social & business, and produce a magazine or newsletter that showed off the local scene via the myriad of creative talents in the Minneapolis area. Consider this, for example. Does AIGA National have any idea what the winters are like in Minnesota? That lakes have an ice cap four feet thick? That maybe those hard ass winters make those creative types more creative because it's a lot warmer hanging around the computer than dealing with the challenge of driving home? A local story idea in their version of ROUGH, produced by the local Minneapolis club with their own identity, quirks, charm, goals, events, auctions, & parties? Something fun? I don't know. What do you think?

AIGA MINNEAPOLIS

If you have turned directly to ROUGHAGE & haven't read "Happy Campers" yet, then go read that & this will make more sense. For those of you interested in attending Design Camp next fall please contact Doug Powell at 612/339-6904. He's the prez of AIGA Minneapolis & knows everything. And Doug, I thank you all for your kindness & comments. It was a great time & I hope we can come back next year.

A few travel tips: if you elect to drive, it's only 7.5 hours from Dallas to Kansas City & 6 hours to Minneapolis, add another 1.5 to Ruttger's Bay Lake Lodge & you're in the heart of Walleye country (that's a very important fish in these parts). Add a little more time if you stop to pee a lot or believe in speed limits. The weather will most likely be beautiful. While most of the inhabitants in this part of the country are very white they do have some soul but are, in general, bad dancers. People actually look forward to winter and have contests jumping snowmobiles over not quite frozen patches of Bay Lake. Common sense seems to be reserved for a group known as "Snowbirds" who jump in their Winnebagos & beat feet for the Texas coast soon after the first frost. Spam is considered a delicacy.

GIVE ME A SIGN

Sure, I pray. Like, give me a sign but don't scare me. O.K.? Atoka, Oklahoma is a place stranger than it's name, which I have used in sentences for at least thirty years, like, gimme atoka that joint. On our way back from Minnesota, Brandi & I pulled into some fastfood joint and on the way out I noticed Christian signage everywhere. The first one slipped by me as we entered town: "Welcome To Atoka", smaller print just below, "We Love Jesus". No problem. But coming out of the burger place, the sign above the parking lot read, "Whataburger & Fries.99 cents", below that, "Praise The Lord". Driving South, the car wash sign, "Spot Free Rinse" and below that, "Christian Fellowship Meeting 9pm". Leaving town, I stopped to photograph what I thought was the last of at least a dozen signs over a two-mile stretch, "Winning Our City For Jesus". But no. The last one read, "Concealed Gun Training Classes". I thought of a word. Intolerance. And I thought of some of our elected leaders that scare the shit out of me, i.e. Dick Armey & Trent Lott. And some weeks after my return, I turned on the news to learn that a young man had been found tied to a split rail fence in Wyoming & beaten into a coma. He was left for dead, which he eventually did in a Denver hospital. He never gained consciousness and he was gay. But, hey, that was his "lifestyle" choice & he was a sinner, right? So who cares? I care. And you better care. And you better pay attention & realize that your vote is as important at the local level as it is nationally. Please vote & throw those narrow-minded, intolerant bastards as for from our city halls, schools, courts & Washington as possible. Amen.

FIFTY CRUM

Don Crum turned fifty last month and, as you can by the photos, he's managed to keep his form in spite of all the years of partying and beer guzzling with his fraternity brothers. Don, who is a past president of the DSVC, is a quiet person. However, beneath that boyish grin & humble demeanor lies one twisted soul: remember the contest put on by a local men's tie shop? Design the most creative tie you can think of? Don's biggest problem was loading his entry into the truck required for delivery of the railroad tie he had decorated. Chili Cookoffs? He certainly must be remembered for his "Mariachi Chili", where he held a mannequin on each side of him, with movable mouths (like on The Conan Show). The faces on the mannequins were strangely familiar. Pirtle & Summerford, I think. Mariachi music blared from a jam box hidden behind Don's tight-fitting mariachi outfit while Don lip synced & the dummies' lips flapped open & shut. The best of all had to be when he teamed up with Eric Johannsen to present "Honeymooner Chili" in living black & white. Don provided us all other reasons to drink beer: "Kamikaze Chili", "Gone With The Wind" and "Chili So Bright Ya Gotta Wear Shades". Happy Birthday, Don. Your humour is good medicine. Keep making us laugh.

PHILSTER

WHATZNU

Bonnie Sterling Joins Gilbert Paper

Bonnie Sterling, formerly with Fraser Papers, has joined Gilbert Paper (a Mead Company) as District Sales Manager for Texas, Oklahoma and Louisiana. Bonnie has worked on the DSVC Dallas Show and Student Show events for a number of years, and now she's signed Gilbert Paper up as a DSVC Sustaining Member-Thanks Bonnie, and welcome to Gilbert. Bonnie met graphic designer Bill Cahan-well known for his award winning annual reports-at the '97 AIGA National Conference and discussed her enthusiasm for DSVC. Thanks again to Bonnie and Gilbert Paper for our great November speaker. Call Bonnie at 972.418.9108.

The Young Company Completes Mavs Annual Report

Bob Young with The Young Company just completed the Dallas Mavericks Foundation Annual Report. And, Vicki (I can talk about myself if I want to) just signed a new client FourWins. They produce cool life-enhancing products for conscious living. Call if you want to know what that means. Info: 214.741.6560.

Dallas Artists' Agents Get Together

Twenty-one Dallas artists' agents met at Ziziki's on Wednesday, September the 30th to enjoy the food and catch up on industry news. Berry Hawkins led a lively agenda put together by the attendees. Among the topics discussed:

1.) Internet use, how to quote art
2.) Day-rates vs per-shot rates, which is fairer to artist and client
3.) Percentage of local vs out-of-town work; what's working, Internet, directories, direct mail?
4.) Stock sales, now that we're all stock agents (likeitornot), how do we price it?

The information pooling proved to be so helpful that the group has decided to get together quarterly. For more information call Andrea or Larry Lynch at 972.761.0500.

Repertoire Changes Name to Repertoire Art

Larry Lynch also reports a company name change to Repertoire Art, and that it's been very busy. John Shipes photographed new Alcon ads for Bates New York, Kevin Rose shots ads for Rhodes Stafford Wines' clients Nokia and ObjectSpace, Amy Bryant illustrated new ads for Kraft Garlic-Flavored Mayonnaise, and Robie Capps flew to LA to shoot record producer Kenny "Babyface" Edmonds for Akai with Chuck Paris (Gilliatt-Paris). Skeeter Hagler shot several projects for The Propel Group, Ben Cornford shot the new Corona Hispanic posters for Montemayor (featuring Playboy's Miss August), Federico Jordán painted Porsches for Brian Niemann at The Boyer Group, Electric Soup worked on the new Cinemark identity program with Jason Brantly of Moroch, and Marc Hausershot new Nortel ads for Temerlin and AMF ads (featuring Michael Jordan) for The Richards Group.

Visit new website, www.RepertoireArt.com with 400+ portfolio images on-line. For more info call Andrea or Larry at 972-761-0500 or contact them through their website.

Stewart Charles Cohen Has A Brush With Crest and Goes On The Road Again With Camry Photographer/Director

Stewart Charles Cohen recently shot five black & white ads for Crest. The series of images shot on location in Dallas will be targeted at the New York and Los Angeles Hispanic market in print, television and outdoor boards for Crest-Hispanic. The agency was Bromley, Aguilar & Associates of San Antonio, Texas. Su Yim, Creative Director; Adriana Ramos-Weardon, Copywriter. Stewart also recently shot two color ads for Toyota Camry. One ad was shot on location in West Texas and one at Dallas Alley in The West ... Saatchi & Saatchi Pacific agency. To see ... Denise Ford at 214.821.6788.

Photographs Do Not Bend Gallery
Dec. 4 - Jan. 16, 1999 Shelby Lee Adams, Appalachian Legacy
Jan. 22 - March 6, 1999 Michael Kenna
Info: 214.969.1852.

Dallas ASMP
Info and upcoming meetings: Jeff Ott 214.638.0602

Jim Myers Busy with Product, Food & Lifestyle

Photographer Jim Myers has been busy with a diverse list of clients. He worked with DDB Needham on a campaign for American Airlines, with Bloom for TGI Friday's (beautiful pasta and hamburger shots), and a product shot for Blockbuster Entertainment. Pete Charbeneau did the digital effects for that one. Melanie Molpus reps Jim Myers, and reports she has added Pete Charbeneau Digital Imaging as a new client. To see Jim or Pete's latest work call Melanie at 214.823.1296.

Sibley/Peteet Design Chosen to Create Paramount's New Logo

Austin, September 25 — The Paramount Theatre for the Performing Arts unveiled its new logo and identity, nicknamed "The Performing P," in the fall 1998 issue of its quarterly newsletter, Paramount Presents. The mark was designed by the Austin office of Texas-based graphic design firm, Sibley/Peteet Design.

In response to the booming interest in the arts in Austin, the Paramount Marketing Committee felt it was time to update the 83-year-old theatre's image. Abbie Rutlege of Rutlege Creative, immediate past chair of the Paramount Marketing Committee, approached Sibley/Peteet Design principal, Rex Peteet, in Spring of 1998 with the challenge. "I felt we were so fortunate to have a nationally-recognized design company in town," says Rutlege. "As soon as they came to Austin I began to think about approaching them to reinvent the Paramount logo. I was lucky. I started with the top design firm and they said yes."

Once charged with the task of designing the new mark, Peteet and his top designers went to work photographing and studying the building's architecture and reading up on its past to give the Paramount a logo based in its rich architectural and artistic history. "When the Paramount asked us to design a new identity for them," says Peteet, "we were thrilled to have the chance to be a part of Austin's history. It's quite an honor to be chosen."

Sibley/Peteet Design, started 16 years ago in Dallas by partners Rex Peteet and Don Sibley, is also known for creating corporate identities for both local and national names, such as Haggar, Mary Kay, Milton Bradley and Shiner Bock, including logos for some of the most visible names in town: GSD&M, Avenue One, GattiTown, Vignette, ChoiceCom, Boundless Technologies and Hand Technologies.

Rough's "WhatzNu" covers industry news, people, and events. So, WhatzNu with you? Pictures are OK, too.
Mail: Vicki Young
1400 Turtle Creek Blvd. #208
Dallas, Texas 75207
Fax: 214.741.6563
email: youngco@flash.net

Calendar of Events

Job Fair
Dallas Show
Student Seminar
Student Show
Brad Holland
Art Auction
Michael Salisbury
Duane Michals
Bill Cahan

STUDIO: HEBE Werbung & Design, Leonberg, Germany **ART DIRECTOR:** Reiner Hebe **DESIGNER:** Simone Rees **PHOTOGRAPHER:** Werner Pawlok **CLIENT/PRODUCT:** Breuninger GmbH & Co./fashion **SOFTWARE:** QuarkXPress **COLORS:** 6, match **PAGES:** 72 **SIZE:** 11 5/16" x 8 7/8" (30.4cm x 22.5cm) **TYPEFACES:** Exquisit, University Medium Expanded **INSPIRATION:** "An exquisite level of design for a presentation of international designers," says the studio. **SPECIAL FEATURES:** Hard covers with concealed wire binding, embossed title, translucent sheets used throughout.

STUDIO: Planet Design Company, Madison, WI **ART DIRECTOR:** Kevin Wade **DESIGNER:** Martha Graettinger **CLIENT/PRODUCT:** Adams Outdoor Advertising/billboards **SOFTWARE:** QuarkXPress, Adobe Illustrator, Adobe Photoshop **PAPER:** Finch Fine, CTI Glama Natural Clear **COLORS:** 4, process plus 1, match **PAGES:** 12 plus cover **SIZE:** 11" x 8½" (28cm x 21.6cm) **PRINT RUN:** 50,000 **COST PER UNIT:** US$1.75 **TYPEFACES:** Interstate Regular, Interstate Bold, Interstate Black **INSPIRATION:** Outdoor advertising. **CONCEPT:** According to designer Martha Graettinger, the idea behind this brochure was "to position outdoor advertising as a creative way to market, and Adams Outdoor Advertising as the creative partner." **SPECIAL FEATURES:** Digitally fuzzed letters on a vellum cover emphasize the piece's fun focus on UFOs and the paranormal.

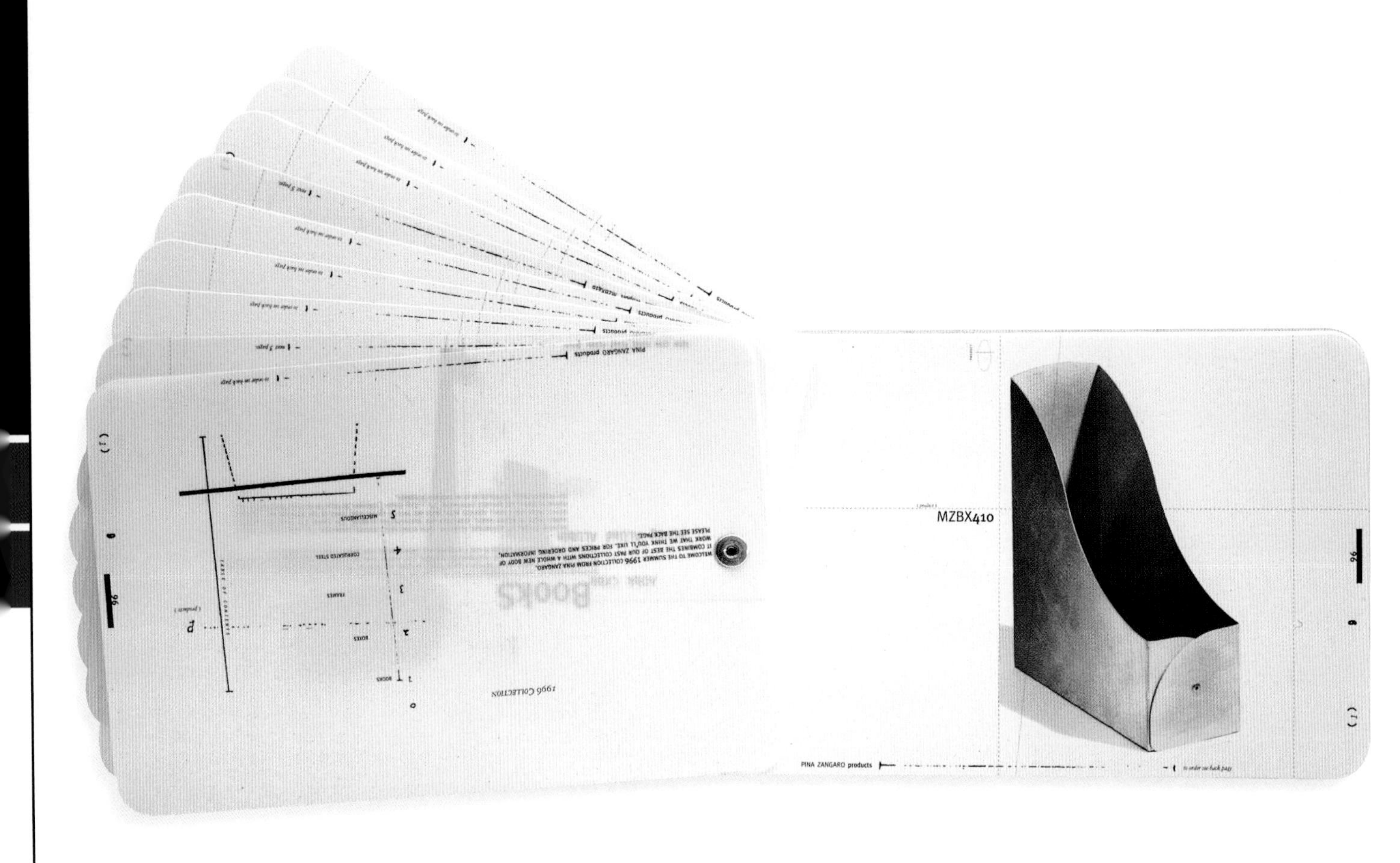

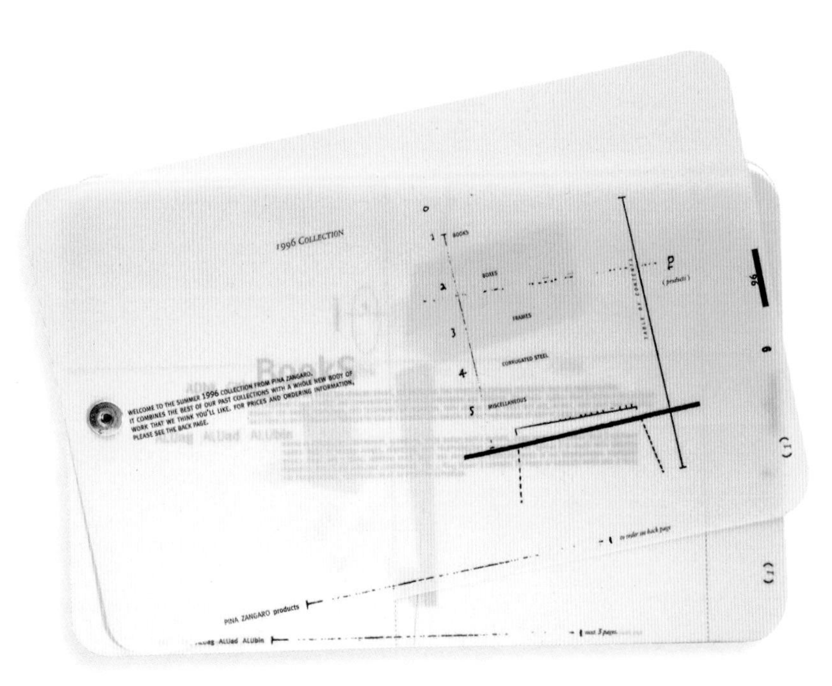

STUDIO: Jennifer Sterling Design, San Francisco, CA **CREATIVE DIRECTOR:** Jennifer Sterling **ILLUSTRATOR:** Jennifer Sterling **WRITER:** Tim Mullen **PHOTOGRAPHER:** Dave Magnusson **TYPOGRAPHER:** Jennifer Sterling **PRINTER:** Logos Graphics **CLIENT/PRODUCT:** Pina Zangaro/product company **PAPER:** Gilbert ESSE Tan, Gilbert Gilclear Cream **COLORS:** Black **PAGES:** 22 **SIZE:** 5 7/16" x 8 1/2" (13.8cm x 21.5cm) **CONCEPT:** "The objective was to create a portfolio of works that reflected Pina Zangaro's design sensibilities and product line," says creative director Jennifer Sterling. "With most of their product line fabricated in various metal materials, a solid die-cut metal cover created an initial cohesiveness. The success of the book was achieved much from a budget perspective, in that the book is modular and can be updated when the development of additional products occur."

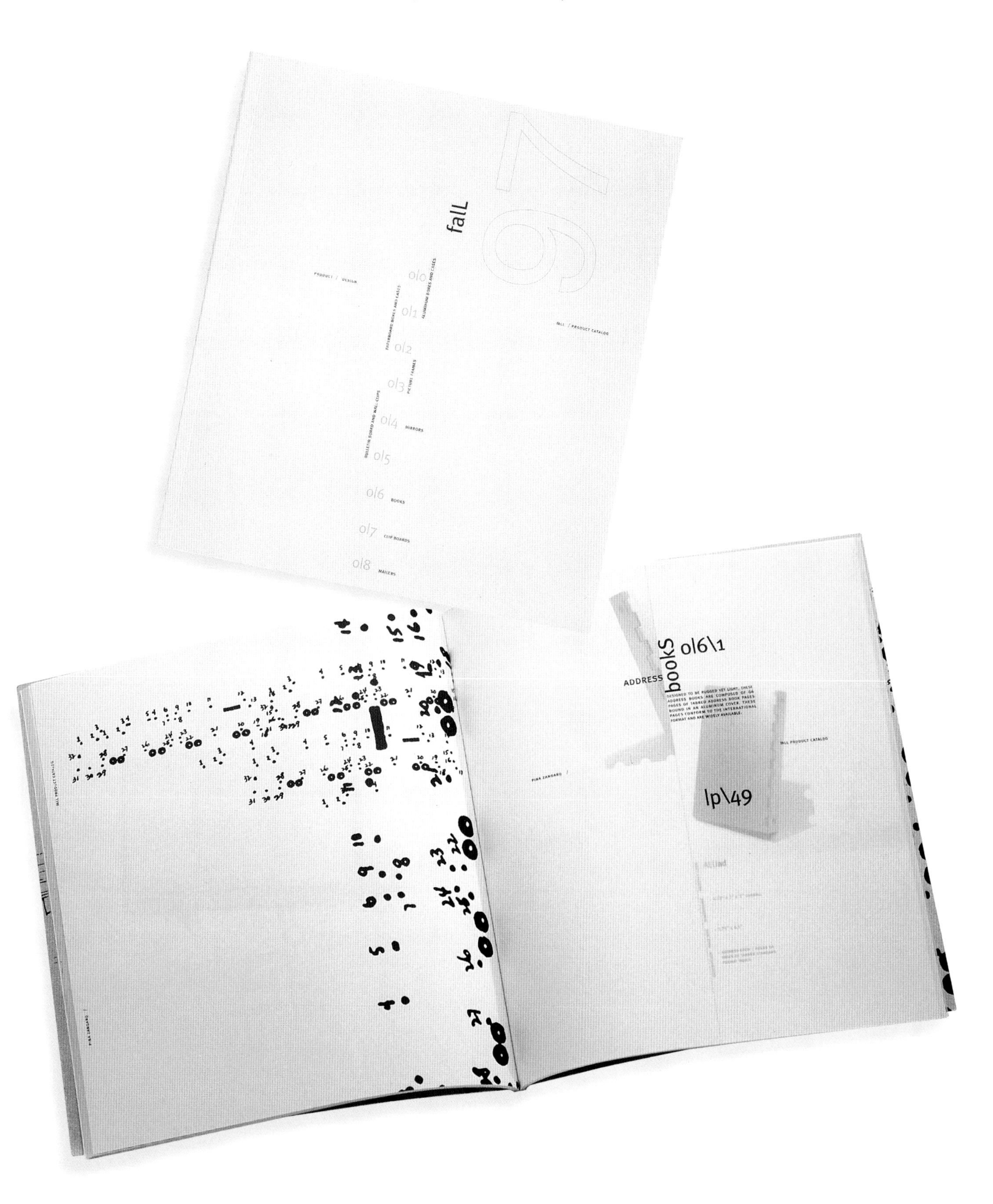

STUDIO: Jennifer Sterling Design, San Francisco, CA **CREATIVE DIRECTOR:** Jennifer Sterling **ILLUSTRATOR:** Jennifer Sterling **WRITER:** Tim Mullen **PHOTOGRAPHER:** Dave Magnusson **TYPOGRAPHER:** Jennifer Sterling **PRINTER:** Logos Graphics **CLIENT/PRODUCT:** Pina Zangaro/product company **PAPER:** Gilbert ESSE Tan, Gilbert Gilclear Cream **COLORS:** 2, black and match metallic silver **PAGES:** 39 **SIZE:** 9" x 8" (22.9cm x 20.3cm) **CONCEPT:** "Layering dividers printed on vellum organized their divisions within each product line," says creative director Jennifer Sterling, "and created a blend between the structural typography and images."

STUDIO: Murphy Design Inc., Cleveland, OH **ART DIRECTOR:** Murphy Design Inc. **DESIGNER:** Mark Murphy **ILLUSTRATOR:** Mark Murphy **CLIENT:** AIGA San Diego **SOFTWARE:** QuarkXPress **PAPER:** Potlatch McCoy Gloss **COLORS:** 4, match plus gloss varnish **SIZE:** 6" x 4½" (15.2cm x 11.5cm) (folded); 6" x 18" (15.2cm x 45.9cm) (unfolded) **PRINT RUN:** 6,000 **COST PER UNIT:** US$0.36 **TYPEFACES:** Bodoni, Dogma, Clarendon, The Mix **INSPIRATION:** Designer Mark Murphy says he allowed himself plenty of time to "play with the photocopier to create interesting texture," creating arresting artwork from a variety of original images. The invitation was also a self-promotion for Murphy, who spoke at the meeting about—self-promotion. **CONCEPT:** "A simple message of fun!" **SPECIAL PRODUCTION TECHNIQUES:** Spot gloss varnish adds subtle texture.

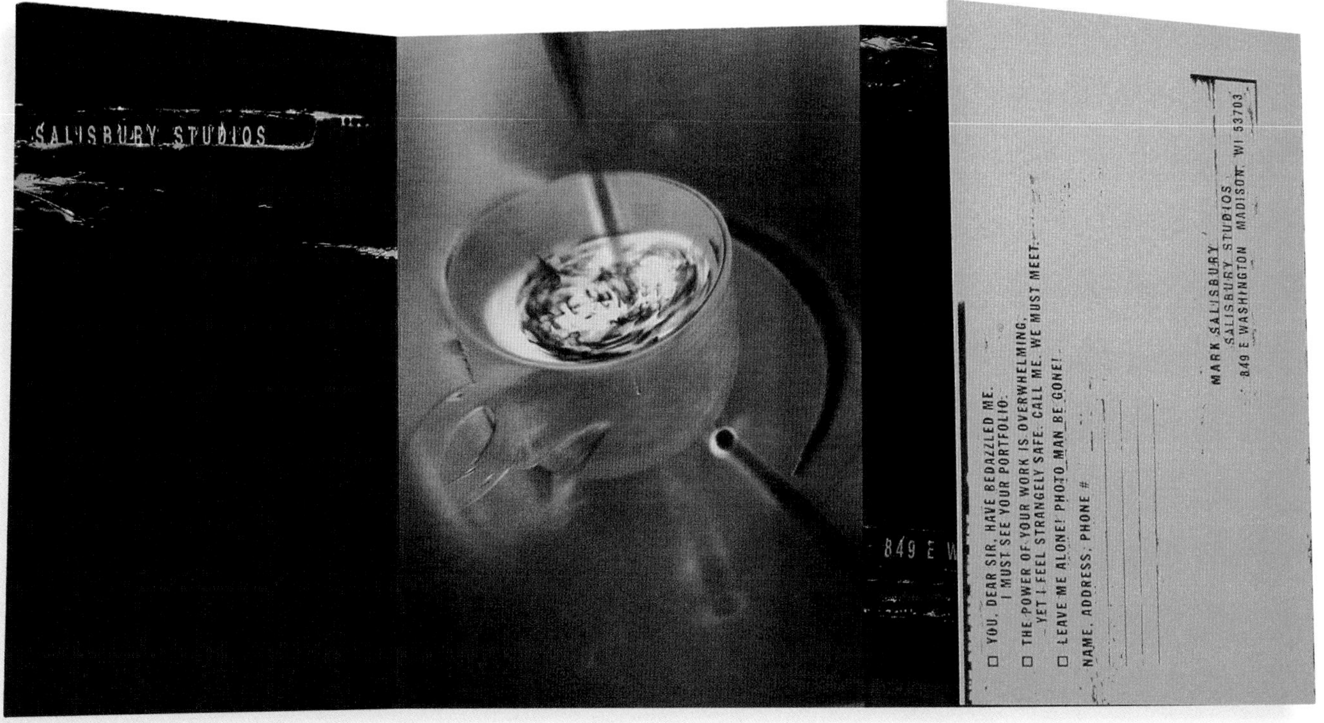

STUDIO: Planet Design Company, Madison, WI **ART DIRECTOR:** Kevin Wade **DESIGNER:** Raelene Mercer **PHOTOGRAPHER:** Mark Salisbury **CLIENT/SERVICE:** Mark Salisbury/photographer **SOFTWARE:** QuarkXPress, Adobe Photoshop **COLORS:** 4, process plus 2, match **SIZE:** 5½" x 3⅞" (14cm x 9.9cm) (folded); 5½" x 15½" (14cm x 39.3cm) (unfolded) **PRINT RUN:** 500 each of 4 **INSPIRATION:** "The photographer's work is very experimental and tactile," says Planet Design. "He works on his images extensively in the darkroom. We wanted to capture some of the qualities surrounding film and print processing, etc." **CONCEPT:** "Show-off photography samples with a little attitude prompting interest in a portfolio showing—this was our goal. Each of the first four mailers can be hole-punched to indicate which of the four has come in the mail. We hoped to generate a 'collect all four' vibe around the campaign." **SPECIAL FEATURES:** "The reply card is perforated for easy tear-and-return." **SPECIAL COST-CUTTING TECHNIQUES:** All four mailers were printed at once, along with business cards.

design +natur
das problem der mischung
Dem Zusammenhalt und Zusammenhang der Dinge liegen die Prinzipien der Materie und Struktur, Passivität und Aktivität zugrunde. Die Einheit des Ganzen beschreibt sich durch immer wieder andere Formen der Mischung. Die stoische Physik geht aus von der Vorstellung eines materiellen Kontinuums als Kosmos. Diese materielle Ganzheit basiert auf zwei Prinzipien: einem aktiven und einem passiven. Das aktive Prinzip wird als das schöpferische Feuer bezeichnet und bildet die alles durchdringende Ursubstanz. Sie gilt als das Prinzip der Spezifikation, der Individuation, der Bewegung, des Bewegungszusammenhangs. Das wirklich Seiende ist für die Stoiker das Körperliche und stellt eine Verbindung zweier materieller Substrate dar, deren Synthese sowohl die Einheit des Ganzen als auch Gestalt, Beschaffenheit, Bewegung , Veränderung erzeugt. Das aktive pneumatische Substrat mit der formenden und bindenden Kraft steht der stofflichen Materie, dem passiven Material gegenüber. Wichtig in diesem Zusammenhang ist die Zuordnung der vier Urelemente: das aktive Substrat setzt sich zusammen aus dem warmen Feuer und der kalten Luft, das passive aus der trockenen Erde und dem feuchten Wasser.
Aus diesem Grundgedanken heraus stellt sich die Frage nach der Erklärung der bunten Vielfältigkeit der Welt. Wie ist die Entwicklung der qualitativen Verschiedenheit der Dinge aus einer Ursubstanz zu denken? Zur Lösung der Problematik stellen die Stoiker die Theorie der verschiedenen Formen von Verbindungen auf. Unterschieden wird in vier Mischgraden.
Paranthesis
Nebeneinanderstellung
Krasis
Durchdringung
Mixis
Mischung
Synchysis
Absolute Vermischung

STUDIO: Fachbereich Design + Medien, Fachhochschule Hannover, Hannover, Germany **ART DIRECTORS:** Bärbel Kühne, Iris Maria vom Hof **DESIGNERS:** design students **SOFTWARE:** QuarkXPress, Adobe Photoshop **PAPER:** Seiler Unbleached, Offset **COLORS:** 4, process plus 8, match **PAGES:** 80 **SIZE:** 8¼" x 5 15/16" (21cm x 15cm) **TYPEFACES:** Palatino (floating text), News Gothic **INSPIRATION:** "design + natur presents the ideas, thoughts and visions of young graphic designers on the topics of design, nature and ecology," says art director Bärbel Kühne. **CONCEPT:** "Based on two main thoughts: 1) Design (and designers) have to take on responsibility toward oneself, and the changes that are necessary for society, and 2) The formation of good taste is as important as the conservation of nature."

Geschmacksbildung ist ebenso wichtig wie Naturschutz
Iris Maria vom Hof
Faktisch gesehen ist unsere gesamte Arbeitswelt in der Hochschule durchzogen von Geschmacksvorstellungen unterschiedlichster Notierung, vom einfachen Mahl in der Mensa bis zum Ausdruck der feinen Geschmacksnuance der Ästhetik-Bildung in Kunst und Design. Ob beim Mundgeschmack oder bei der Ästthetik-Debatte, wer Verschiedenheit addiert und nicht vermischt oder trennt, der braucht sich auch um den Sinn des Geschmacks am Leben nicht zu sorgen. Und was wäre für unsere Arbeit in den kreativen Gestaltungsbereichen vernünftiger, als den eigenen Lebensstil und die individuelle Lebenssicht zu pflegen? Schon aus Selbsterhaltungstrieb sollten wir Augenmenschen „hoch zwei" exemplarisch alle Grundqualitäten des Ges
übertragenen Sinn aktivieren: Neben Süß – und damit immer unwidersp
auch Sauer, Salzig und Bitter. Die pittoreske Geschma
ders nahrhaft aus allen vier Temperamenten.
Geschmack als Gaumenfreude oder Geschmack als
kreist immer um das Bekenntnis, wie Menschen leben
logie-Krise und Naturschutz. Die Müsli-Askese und
bewußten Generation ebenso wie der momenta
essentieller Genußqualität bestätigen nach wie
Lösungsweg. Der Restmüll im Kopf ist damit noch
ge die isolierte Diktatur der menschlichen Konsum
Naturschutz, besser gesagt: von Naturverständ
Weniger-statt-Mehr-Kompromiß ist der Ablaß k
Das Projekt Design und Natur betont deshalb d
Aspekt der Eigenwahrnehmung durch Sinn
der herkömmlichen Divergenz von Ökologi
Ästhetik- und Naturdebatte richtet sich dementsprechend auf die Wahrnehmung und Untersuchung innerer Einstellungen und setzt Geschmacksbildung in Bezug zu einem mitweltbewußten, zukunftsfähigeren Lebensstil.
Es gibt nichts Falsches im wahren Leben oder nach Adorno: „Es gibt kein wahres Leben im Falschen." Die Geschmacksfrage wird immer polyphon zu beantworten sein – Abgrenzungen können wir beim Goldwaschen von Gestaltungsideen am wenigsten gebrauchen. Wer den Claim zu eng absteckt, der wird in seinem Sieb über kurz oder lang immer wieder den gleichen Sand rütteln. Darüber hinaus birgt das Geschmacksthema eine weitreichendere Brisanz, als das Roulette der Glückssuche vermuten läßt; es geht
diskutiert wird, immer dann, wenn in Kunst und Gestal
beurteilt wird, was gut und
wort und sinne
In einer Zeit, in der das morgendliche Duschen, das heruntergeschlungene Frühstück und Auf-die-Toilette-gehen, das Streicheln und Füttern des Haustieres, Schnell-noch-die-Blumen-gießen und der zweimalwöchentliche Geschlechtsakt unsere letzten alltäglichen natürlichen Handlungen sind, das Gespräch über das Wetter, die Urlaubslandschaft und das Tuscheln hinter vorgehaltener Hand über die Tabus Krankheit und Tod unsere einzige Kommunikation über Natur sind, kann man seine Mitmenschen kaum zum Umdenken und Umfühlen bewegen.
Die genaue Betrachtung der Zwiebelhaut erfordert eine Selbstdisziplin und Form von Geduld, die wir eigentlich verlernt haben. Wenn wir uns der Zwiebelhaut nun wieder hingeben, so ist unser schlechtes Gewissen beruhigt, nicht weil wir uns selbstkritisch mit unserem persönlichen konsumistischen Verhalten beschäftigt haben, sondern weil wir die Disziplin aufgebracht haben, uns mit Natur etwas länger als sonst zu beschäftigen. Diese Erfahrung läßt uns uns gut fühlen. Aber was schafft sie darüber hinaus? Verhilft sie uns, die verlorene Einheit mit der Natur wieder zu erlangen und dann mehr Verantwortung zu übernehmen? Vielleicht spiegelt sich darin nur die alte Sichtweise, nämlich die der erhabenen Natur: „Ach, guck mal, wie durchdacht und präzise selbst eine Zwiebel gewachsen ist." An den Kern der Zwiebel gelangen wir nicht, denn unsere Augen fangen an zu brennen. Die sinnliche Erfahrung der Zwiebel wird zur Qual.
Auch heute noch – oder schon wieder –
Du magst die
ganz

STUDIO: Mires Design Inc., San Diego, CA **ART DIRECTOR:** John Ball **DESIGNER:** Deborah Hom **ILLUSTRATOR:** Miguel Perez **CLIENT/SERVICE:** Anacomp/information management and retrieval **PAPER:** Potlatch Eloquence **COLORS:** 4, process plus 2, match **PAGES:** 6 plus cover **SIZE:** 8 ½" x 11" (21.6cm x 28cm) **TYPEFACES:** Futura, Times Roman **INSPIRATION:** "Anacomp's business is information," says art director John Ball. "We designed this piece of information to be both functional and accessible." **CONCEPT:** "The style guide was designed as a tool to help both internal and external audiences implement Anacomp's new identity. To encourage compliance, we kept the guidelines simple and direct, with the design accessible and engaging. Swatches were provided for Anacomp's corporate color, with a secondary color palette provided in PMS, CMYK and RGB."

STUDIO: Gee + Chung Design, San Francisco, CA **ART DIRECTOR:** Earl Gee **DESIGNERS:** Earl Gee, Fani Chung **PHOTOGRAPHER:** Scott Peterson **CLIENT/SERVICE:** Communications Ventures/venture capital for early-stage communications and networking companies **SOFTWARE:** QuarkXPress, Adobe Illustrator, Adobe Photoshop **PAPER:** Strathmore Writing Laid Soft White Cover (cover); S.D. Warren Co. Lustro Dull Cream Cover (interior) **COLORS:** 2, foil stamping plus 2, match (cover); 4, process plus metallic and gloss varnish (interior) **PAGES:** 12 plus cover **SIZE:** 7" x 11" (17.8cm x 28cm) **PRINT RUN:** 2,500 **COST PER UNIT:** US$10.19 **TYPEFACE:** Sabon family (Adobe) **INSPIRATION:** For the cover, says designer Earl Gee, the idea was "freezing a frame of time, conveying information floating past the viewer. The essence of what ComVen does is put things together: ideas, technology, finances and people. Our concept was networking, an ideal theme to relate to both the communications and venture capital industries." **CONCEPT:** "Typical venture capital brochures tend to be tall, slim books with dark, textured covers; soft, warm text pages; and photos of wood-paneled desks and bookshelves. We wanted to break the mold and let the ideas of our dynamic client take center stage. As telecommunications today is about the exponential growth in bandwidth, a long horizontal format seemed appropriate," Gee explains. Headlines printed in gold metallic ink introduce each new idea. Photography, Gee says, was a challenge. "For 'The Next Big Thing,' we created an out-of-focus photograph of a few lumps of clay attached to a bundle of copper wires. It worked beautifully; nobody could really say what it was." **SPECIAL TYPE TECHNIQUES:** The company name is spelled out in various networking configurations, to reinforce the theme. **SPECIAL PRODUCTION TECHNIQUES:** The cover is blind-embossed and foil-stamped. **SPECIAL FEATURES:** A custom die-cut pocket is shaped like a transistor.

ART DIRECTOR/DESIGNER: Philip Fass **CLIENT/SERVICE:** Harvey Hess/music critic, librettist, educator **SOFTWARE:** Macromedia FreeHand, QuarkXPress **PAPER:** Neenah Ultra (cards), tracing paper (wrapper), tiny stickers (to secure wrapper) **COLORS:** Process black **PAGES:** 6 **SIZE:** 5" x 5" (12.8cm x 12.8cm) **PRINT RUN:** 300 **COST PER UNIT:** US$1.30 **TYPEFACES:** Aurea Inline, Author, Helvetica Inserat-Roman, Franklin Gothic Heavy, Aurea Titling, Künstler Script Medium, Madrone, Helvetica, Trajan Regular **INSPIRATION:** According to professor and designer Philip Fass, "The inspiration was the music, in that the patterns generated evoke classical music. Ideally, the recipient has an aesthetic experience that builds expectation for the performance. I also like linear design motifs (topographic maps, certain kinds of diagrams in physics textbooks, the veins on a leaf, etc.). Also, the motif used is an attempt to answer the question, 'What is the shape of music?' (although it's probably only a partial answer). The forms become volumetric as they compress and expand, mirroring the aural quality of this sort of music and filling the available space." **CONCEPT:** "This was the ninth in a series of concerts held at the Hess home, and they have become real events in the community. So I was hoping to give recipients both the experience of mere information (the stick-on tab had all the pertinent information) and the experience of the aesthetic (the individual cards). Through this juxtaposition the two experiences are made clearer." **SPECIAL PRODUCTION TECHNIQUES:** The designs printed in black on the reverse of the creamy translucent sheets appear a metallic gray. "Careful registration was needed to back up the design on both sides," says Fass. "The piece was printed by a local Quick Print Shop, Karen's Print Rite. I am grateful to them for tolerating my expectations."

STUDIO: Michael Gunselman Incorporated, Wilmington, DE **ART DIRECTOR/DESIGNER:** Michael Gunselman **PHOTOGRAPHER:** Ed Cunicelli **CLIENT/SERVICE:** Ed Cunicelli/photography **SOFTWARE:** Adobe PageMaker **PAPER:** Consort Royal Silk **COLORS:** 2, match **PAGES:** 32 **SIZE:** 4½" x 3½" (11.4cm x 8.9cm) **PRINT RUN:** 500 **COST PER UNIT:** US$6 **TYPEFACES:** Adobe Garamond Expert, Bembo Small Caps, Zapf Dingbats **INSPIRATION:** "To create a self-promotional brochure featuring the photography in a clean, simple format with minimal copy," says designer Michael Gunselman. **CONCEPT:** "The small, jewel-like format would distinguish this brochure from among the many promotional items received by targeted designers and art directors." **SPECIAL COST-CUTTING TECHNIQUES:** "The small size allowed more images from the photographer's portfolio to be included."

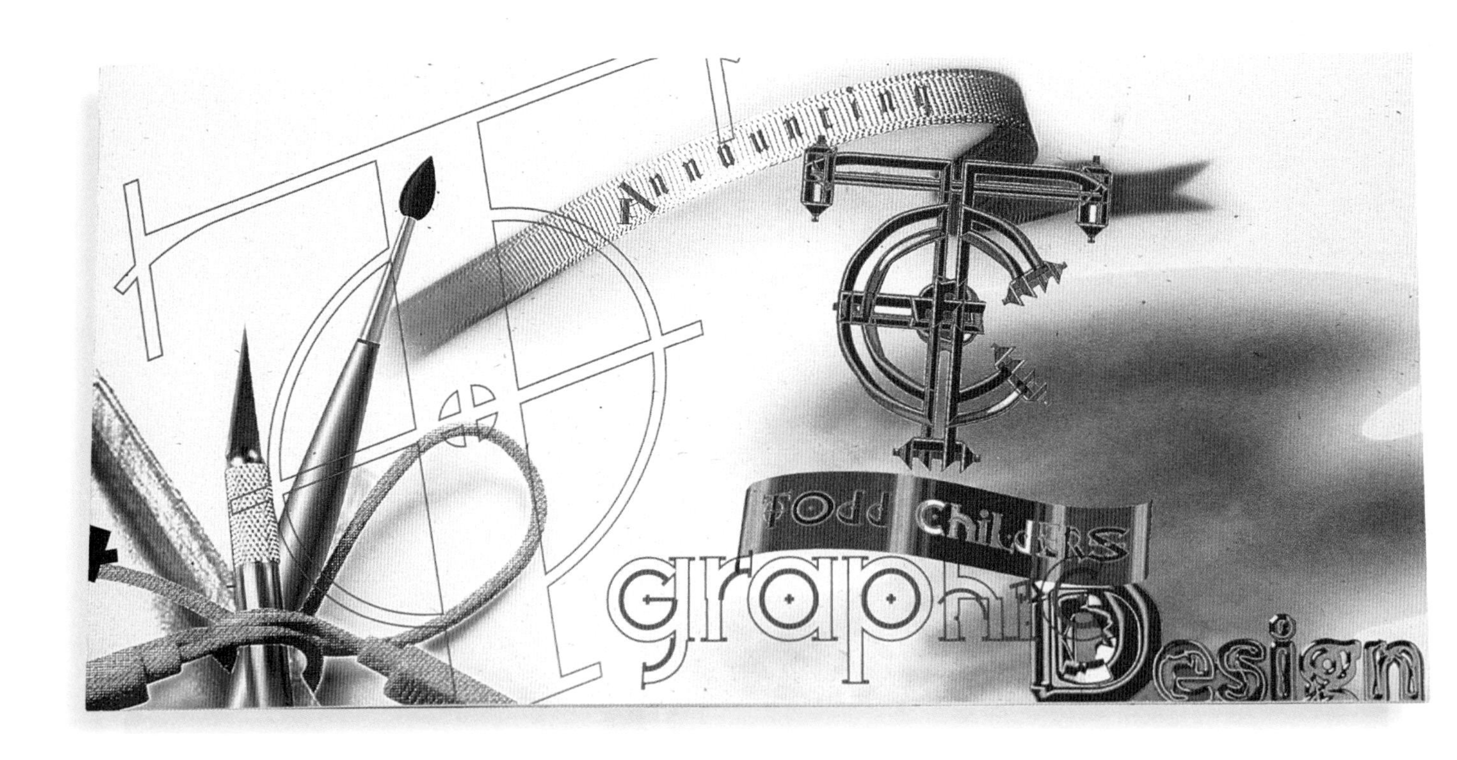

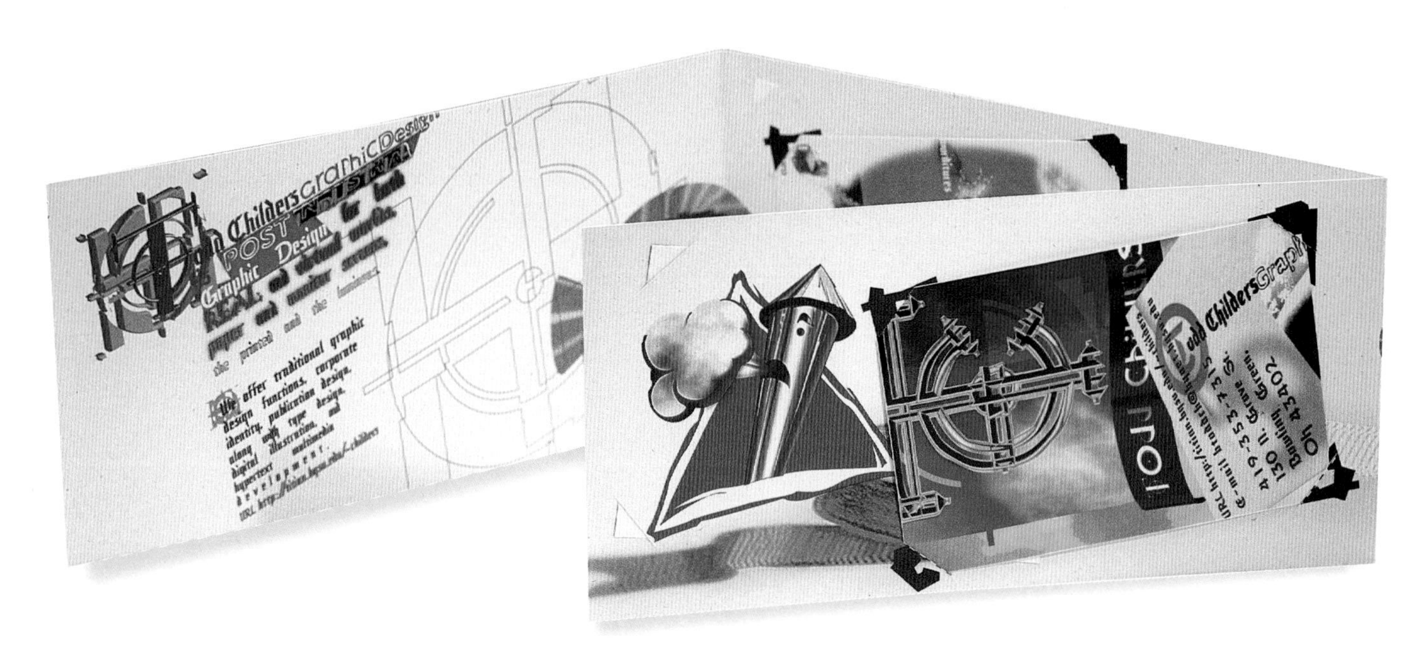

STUDIO: For Eyes Media (formerly Todd Childers Graphic Design), Bowling Green, OH **ART DIRECTOR:** Todd Childers **DESIGNER:** Todd Childers **ILLUSTRATOR:** Todd Childers **PHOTOGRAPHER:** Todd Childers **CLIENT:** Self **SOFTWARE:** Adobe Illustrator, Adobe Photoshop, Macromedia Fontographer **PAPER:** French Speckletone Milkweed **COLORS:** 2, match (full-color photographic images are tipped in) **SIZE:** 4" x 8⅜" (10.2cm x 21.3cm)(folded); 4" x 24 15/16" (10.2cm x 63.3cm)(unfolded) **PRINT RUN:** 500 **TYPEFACES:** Burnout (Todd Childers), Fraktura (Todd Childers), Usher (Todd Childers) **INSPIRATION:** Old-time postcard albums. **CONCEPT:** "The individual icons used in my design are based on a graduate project at CalArts." **SPECIAL TYPE TECHNIQUES:** "To make a font, I use Adobe Illustrator for my initial drawings and Macromedia Fontographer for the final drawings and all of my production work." **SPECIAL PRODUCTION TECHNIQUES:** "Duotones stretch a two-color budget." **SPECIAL FOLDS OR FEATURES:** Tipped-in photos. "This saves money and allows me to customize each mailing." **SPECIAL COST-CUTTING TECHNIQUES:** "The 'die' cuts are individually cut by me."

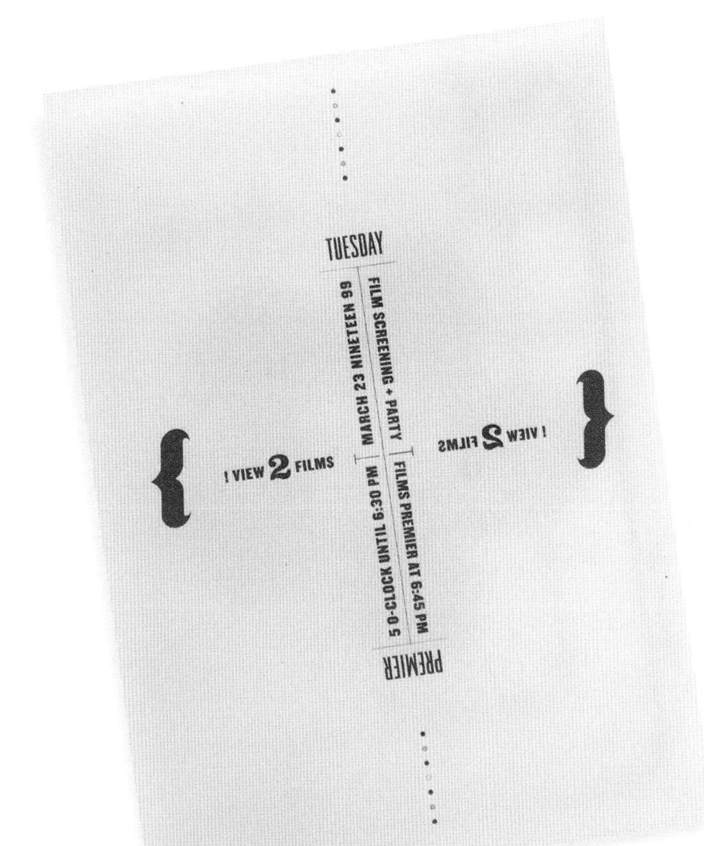

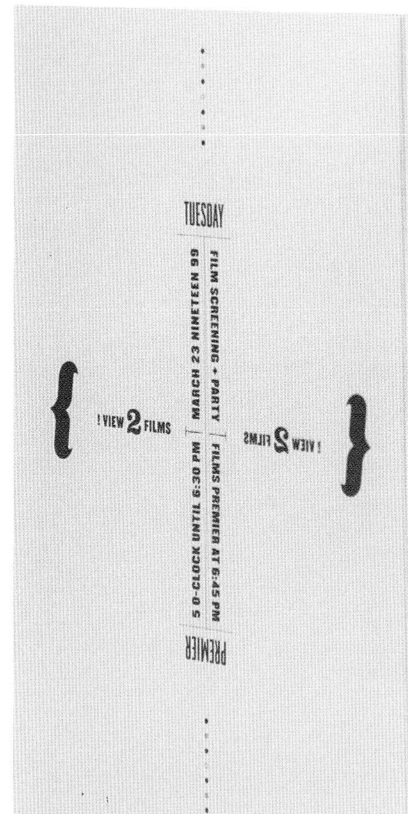

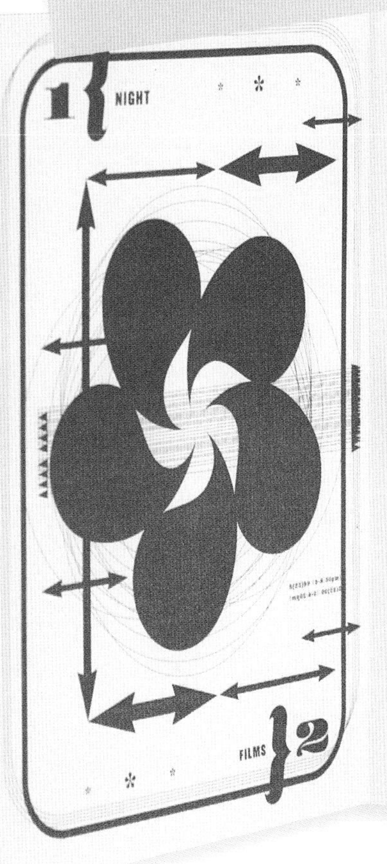

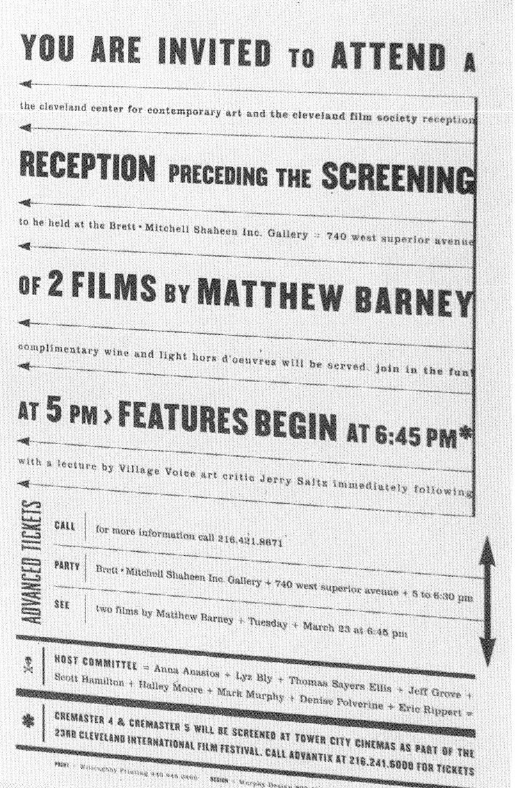

STUDIO: Murphy Design Inc., Cleveland, OH **ART DIRECTOR:** Murphy Design Inc. **DESIGNER:** Mark Murphy **CLIENT/SERVICE:** Cleveland Center for Contemporary Art/nonprofit foundation **SOFTWARE:** QuarkXPress, Macromedia FreeHand **COLORS:** 1, match **SIZE:** 7" x 5" (17.9cm x 12.7cm)(folded); 7" x 15" (17.9cm x 38.1cm)(unfolded) **INSPIRATION:** "A low budget, fast turnaround and immediate need," says designer Mark Murphy. **CONCEPT:** "Using paper to satisfy the need for interesting texture by the play of natural light and ink."

STUDIO: Prototype 21, London, U.K. **ART DIRECTOR:** Prototype 21 **DESIGNER:** Prototype 21 **ILLUSTRATOR:** Prototype 21 **CLIENT/SERVICE:** Self/graphic design, clothing label, garment printing **SOFTWARE:** CorelDRAW, Photopaint, Adobe Photoshop, Macromedia Fontographer **PAPER:** 130 Silk **COLORS:** 4, process (stickers); 4, process plus 1, match metallic (poster) **SIZE:** 4$\frac{13}{16}$" x 4$\frac{13}{16}$" (12.3cm x 12.3cm)(brochure); 2$\frac{1}{16}$" x 2$\frac{7}{8}$" (5.1cm x 7.3cm)(each sticker) **PRINT RUN:** 1,000 **COST PER UNIT:** UK£0.77 **TYPEFACES:** AO (Prototype 21); Automa Sport (Prototype 21); Euro 2000 (Prototype 21); various Japanese, Arabic, Tibetan, Thai and Korean faces (Prototype 21); Comic Sans MS (Microsoft); Empire Builder (Benn Coifman); VAG Rounded BT (Bitstream Inc.) **INSPIRATION:** "Pan-global information overspill," says designer Paul Nicholson. "A multicultural, high velocity, head-on collision. Death to retro!" **CONCEPT:** "To communicate the scope of thought and ideas at Prototype 21." **SPECIAL TYPE TECHNIQUES:** "AO, Automa Sport and Euro 2000 started life as pencil on paper, the roughs being scanned and the vector graphic created for each character using Macromedia Fontographer. With the non-English text, I had words and sentences translated. The works are typographical pieces, in that I did not create a full alphabet. Readability is a consideration; however, the primary objective is form. In many respects I see the work in a similar vein to graffiti art or tagging."

P21 - Issue One
P21
ПРОТОТИП ДВАДЦАТЬ ОДИН
ПРОТОТИП 21
MULTI LINGUAL TYPOGRAPHY AND CALLIGRAPHY
DESIGNED AT PROTOTYPE 21 TYPE FOUNDRY
メイドインUK

Although type can sometimes replicate the power of spoken words, an image can transcend them. It's often literally possible to say with one picture what it would take—well, you know how many words—to explain.

[image]

[image] 2

in this chapter, images speak volumes. you'll see how:

- A London design firm used details of photos of a half-finished museum to suggest the power and character of its architecture.
- Art Chantry used a photocopier to turn the vice of a low-cost printing method into an artistic virtue.
- Designers at Miriello Graphico transformed found objects from the office into a year's worth of friendly faces, creating a calendar of images clients could display in a handy compact disc jewel case.

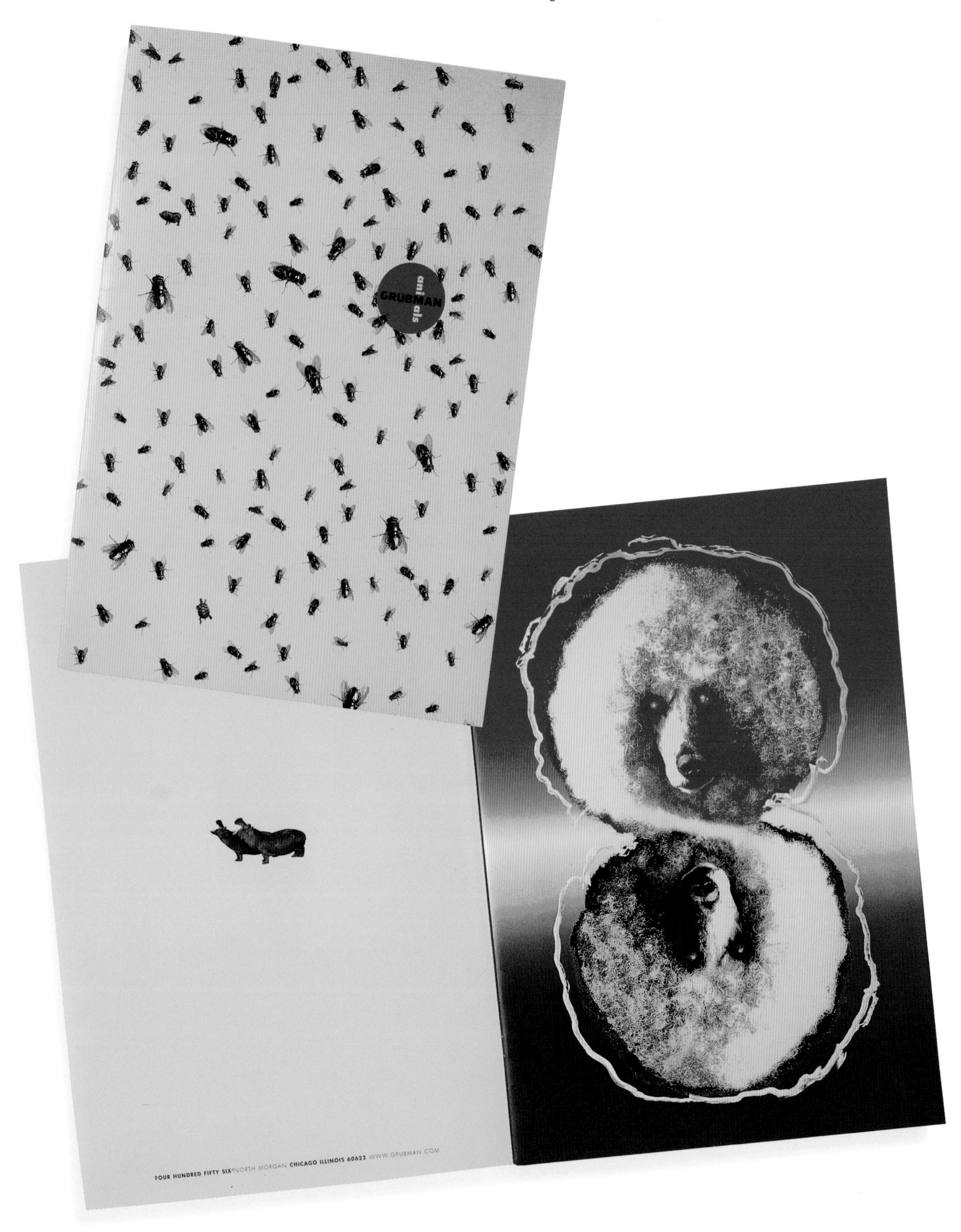

STUDIO: Liska + Associates, Inc., Chicago, IL **ART DIRECTOR:** Steve Liska **DESIGNER:** Andrea Wener **PHOTOGRAPHER:** Steve Grubman **CLIENT:** Grubman Photography **SOFTWARE:** Adobe Photoshop, QuarkXPress **PAPER:** Sappi/S.D. Warren Strobe Text **COLORS:** 4, process plus 2, match **PAGES:** 12 plus cover **SIZE:** 16" x 11" (40.6cm x 27.9cm) **PRINT RUN:** 6,000 **COST PER UNIT:** US$6 **TYPEFACE:** Futura **CONCEPT:** Design Manager Kim Fry says the concept was "to gather Grubman's trademark animal photography into a publication and demonstrate the breadth of the studio's work." A second objective was to show Grubman's expertise in digital manipulation and retouching. **SPECIAL FEATURES:** High gloss paper and superb printing bring out the unique details (fragile wings, supple fur, gleaming scales) that are an important part of animal photography. Takeoffs of famous posters add a humorous note.

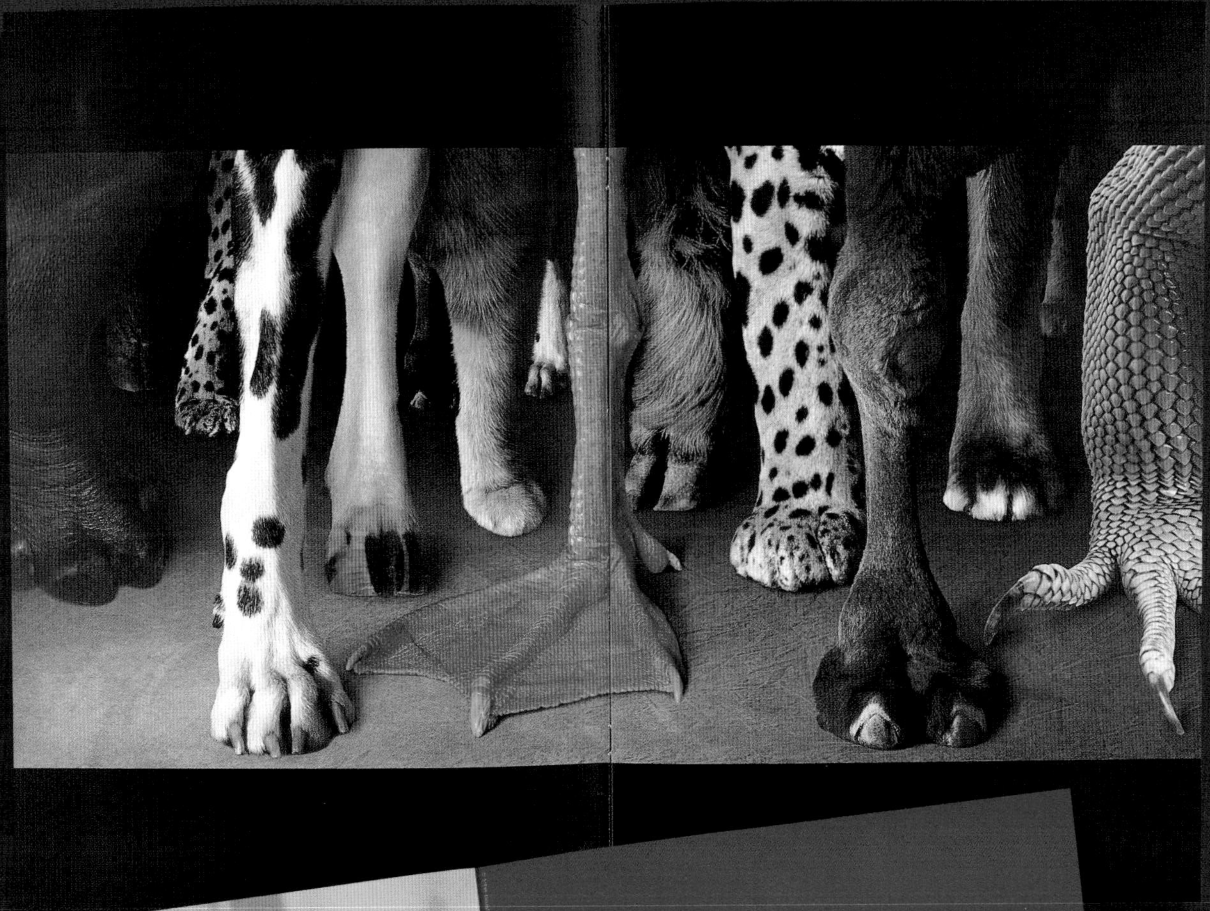

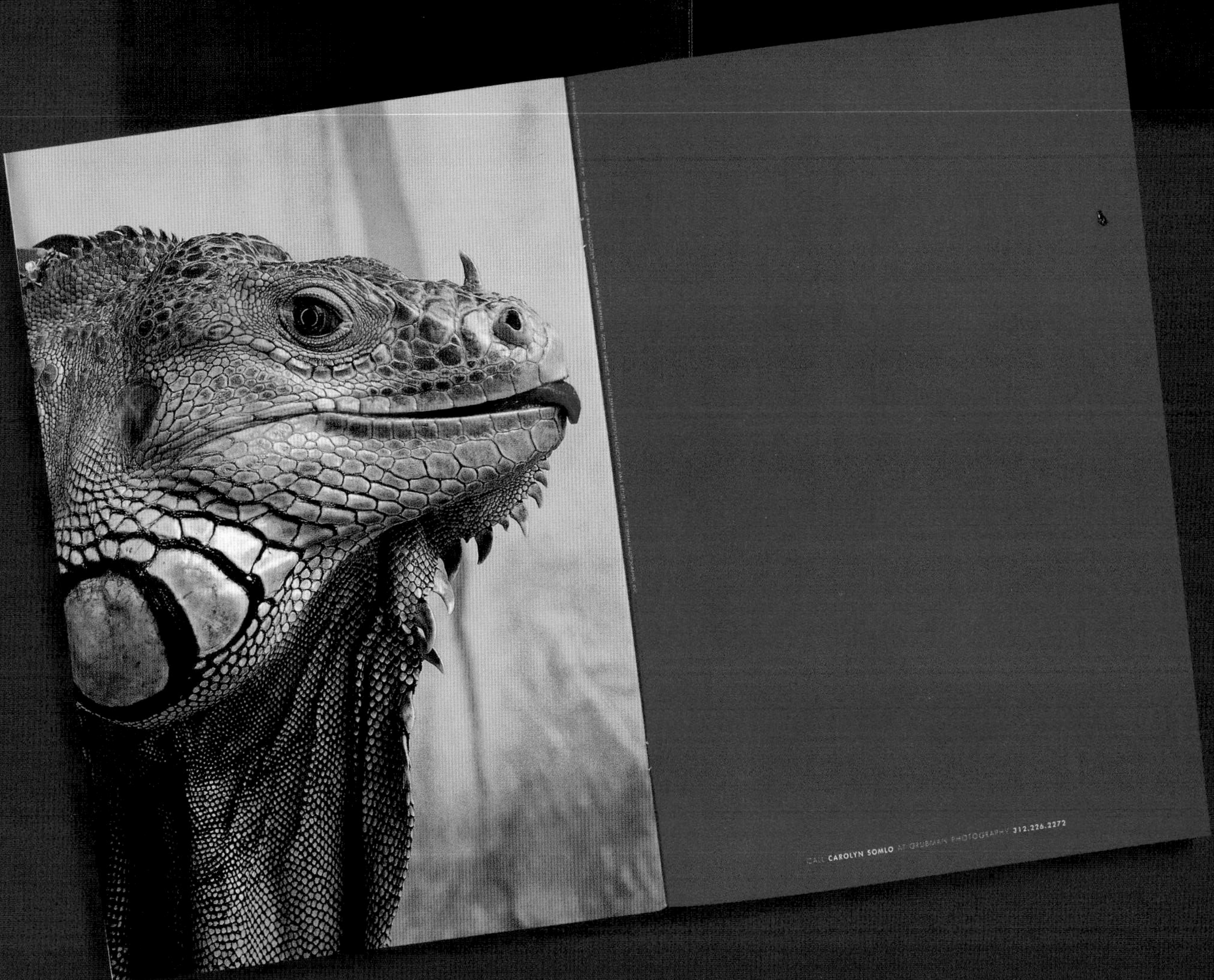
CALL CAROLYN SOMLO AT GRUBMAN PHOTOGRAPHY 312.226.2272

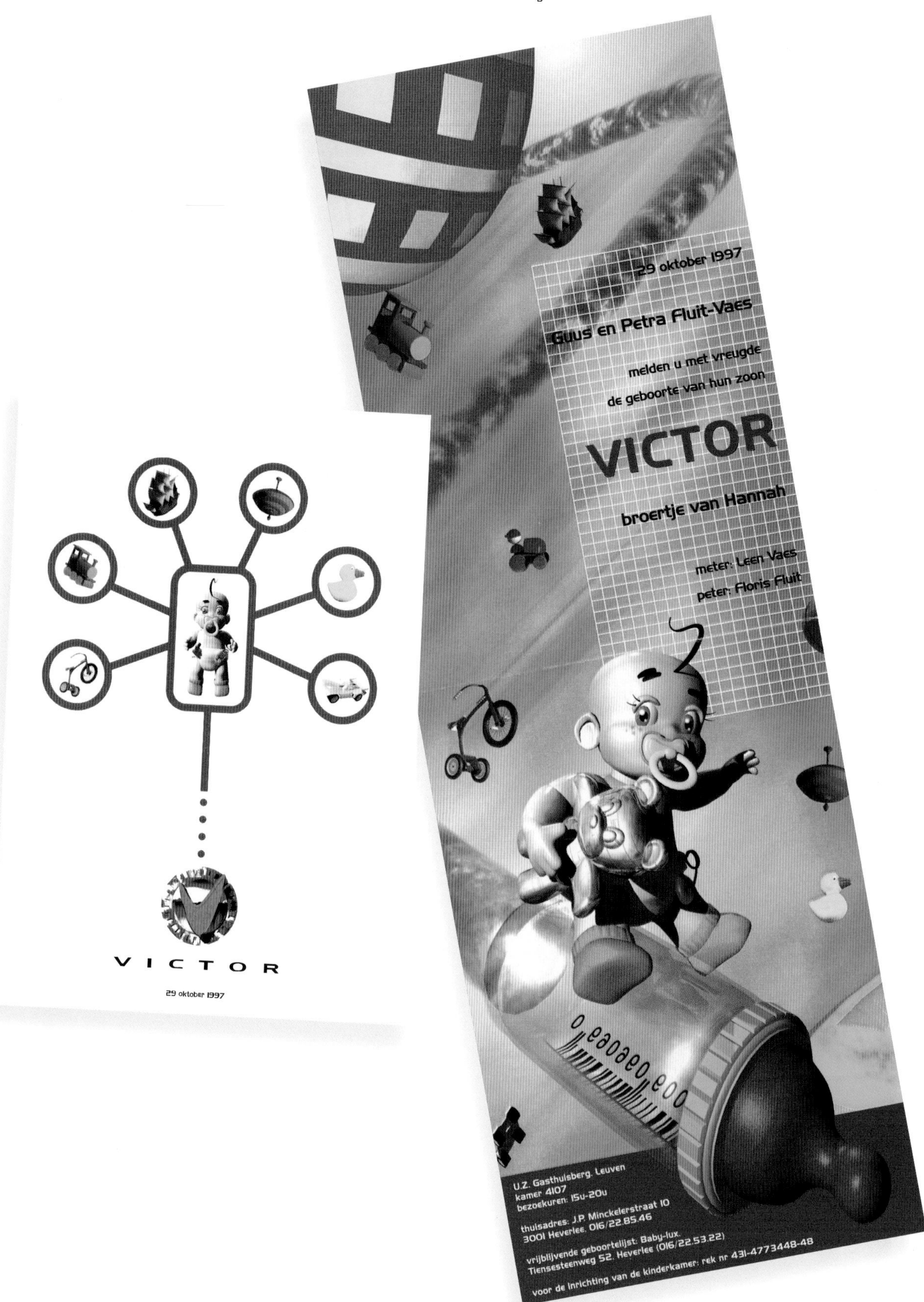

29 oktober 1997
Guus en Petra Fluit-Vaes
melden u met vreugde
de geboorte van hun zoon
VICTOR
broertje van Hannah
meter: Leen Vaes
peter: Floris Fluit
U.Z. Gasthuisberg, Leuven
kamer 4107
bezoekuren: 15u-20u
thuisadres: J.P. Minckelerstraat 10
3001 Heverlee. 016/22.85.46
vrijblijvende geboortelijst: Baby-lux
Tiensesteenweg 52, Heverlee (016/22.53.22)
voor de inrichting van de kinderkamer: rek nr 431-4773448-48
VICTOR
29 oktober 1997

STUDIO: Seven Productions, Kontich, Belgium **ART DIRECTOR:** Sven Mastbooms **DESIGNERS:** Sven Mastbooms, Jeroen van Omme (3-D) **ILLUSTRATORS:** Sven Mastbooms, Jeroen van Omme (3-D art) **CLIENT:** Guus and Petra Fluit-Vaes **SOFTWARE:** Adobe Illustrator, Adobe Photoshop, Lightwave, QuarkXPress **PAPER:** Colorcopy **COLORS:** 4, digital print (Xeikon) **PAGES:** 4 (one sheet) **SIZE:** 11 ½" x 7 ⅞" (29.1cm x 20.1cm) (folded) **CONCEPT:** "Creating a 'baby universe' in which Victor would be the star." **INSPIRATION:** "Stuff important to a baby (toys) relating to a few elements (milk bottle and the metallic bear) that were used on a record sleeve we designed for a group called Eden," says designer Sven Mastbooms. "The 'father,' Guus, signed the group at EMI Music Belgium. The 'V' initial on the cover was inspired by the *Star Trek* logos." **SPECIAL PRODUCTION TECHNIQUE:** 3-D software creates a unique look for the illustrations, which seem to revolve around Baby Victor and his bottle-rocket-like asteroids.

[image]

STUDIO: Mires Design Inc., San Diego, CA **ART DIRECTOR:** José A. Serrano **DESIGNERS:** José A. Serrano, Eric Freedman **PHOTOGRAPHER:** Carl Vanderschuit **CLIENT:** Vanderschuit Photography **SOFTWARE:** Adobe Illustrator **COLORS:** 4, process (interior); 2, match (cover) **PAGES:** 8 plus cover **SIZE:** 11" x 8" (28cm x 20.5cm) **PRINT RUN:** 5,000 **TYPEFACES:** New Baskerville Expert Bold Italic, Helvetica Black **INSPIRATION:** "The simplicity and bold colors of the photography," says art director José A. Serrano. **CONCEPT:** "The purpose of this mailer was to showcase a new style of photography in a fresh way, without too much copy. This way, the visuals were able to speak for themselves." **SPECIAL FEATURES:** Die-cut circles in the cover reveal the client's name, printed on the interior.

STUDIO: Base Art Co., Columbus, OH **ART DIRECTOR/DESIGNER:** Terry Alan Rohrbach **ILLUSTRATOR:** Brandon C. Rohrbach **PHOTOGRAPHERS:** Rick Weber, Cosmo* **CLIENT/SERVICE:** Columbus Society of Communicating Arts/graphic design club **SOFTWARE:** QuarkXPress, Adobe Photoshop **PAPER:** Coronado **COLORS:** 4, process (cover); 1, match plus black (interior) **PAGES:** 106 **SIZE:** 7" x 5 1/4" (17.8cm x 13.4cm) **PRINT RUN:** 1,000 **COST PER UNIT:** US$5 **TYPEFACES:** MGrotesque, Linotype Didot **CONCEPT:** "Developed pro bono, the concept for this piece really came out of the low production budget," says designer Terry Alan Rohrbach. "All art needed to be scanned in-house and Base Art Co. would be responsible for any additional fees. Therefore, accent imagery was created by using selected pieces from the show and converting them into high-contrast art. Also, using a single PhotoDisc photo for the cover enabled us to download the image for a minimal fee. This image was then manipulated in Photoshop to develop the 'round of applause' icon used on the cover and throughout the catalog." **INSPIRATION:** "During my son's Cub Scout meeting, the inspiration for the cover was presented before me as a hundred or so kids simultaneously gave a literal 'round of applause' to the evening's honorees!" **SPECIAL COST-CUTTING TECHNIQUES:** Award winners were photographed in black-and-white Polaroid film, and Base Art Co. scanned the art in-house. Additional accent images were created by converting parts of show photos into high-contrast art.

STUDIO: Nielinger & Rohsiepe Design, Bochum, Germany **ART DIRECTOR:** Nielinger & Rohsiepe Design **DESIGNER:** Herbert Rohsiepe **PHOTOGRAPHER:** Christian Nielinger **CLIENT/PRODUCT:** Sender Schaltanlagen/switchgear fabrication **SOFTWARE:** Adobe Photoshop, Macromedia FreeHand **COLORS:** 4, process plus match silver metallic and matte and gloss varnishes **PAGES:** 8 **SIZE:** 11¾" x 8¼" (29.7cm x 20.9cm) **PRINT RUN:** 1,000 **TYPEFACES:** Thesis Sans Light, Thesis Serif Extra Bold **INSPIRATION:** "The circle and color of the company logo, and the colors and structure of the building—red and silver," says designer Herbert Rohsiepe. **CONCEPT:** "To show a rather visually unattractive product from a special and emotional point of view, on a high-quality level." Distinctive, colorful photographs featuring product details contrast with the large, white pages. Small blocks of type set around a curve punctuate the clean layout. **SPECIAL FEATURE:** The distinctive staples add visual interest.

STUDIO: EAI/Atlanta, Atlanta, GA **CREATIVE DIRECTOR:** Matt Rollins **DESIGNERS:** Matt Rollins, Todd Simmons, Lea Nichols **PHOTOGRAPHER:** Ken Schles **CLIENT:** Appleton Papers **SOFTWARE:** QuarkXPress, Adobe Illustrator **PAPER:** Appleton Utopia Premium Blue White Dull, Cover and Text **COLORS:** 4, process plus match silver metallic and varnish **PAGES:** 16 **SIZE:** 11⅜" x 8½" (29cm x 21.6cm) **TYPEFACE:** Helvetica Neue **INSPIRATION:** According to creative director Matt Rollins: "1) Driving past a blank billboard on I-85 in Atlanta, and 2) nodding in and out of a Philosophy 101 class on John Locke back in college." Rollins notes that "John Locke's essay is 748 pages long. We skipped over the boring parts." **CONCEPT:** Utopia paper as a blank slate. "In 1690, Locke penned a lengthy treatise entitled 'An Essay Concerning Human Understanding,' in which he established the idea of tabula rasa, or 'blank slate.' Locke claimed (controversially) that ideas are not innate. We begin with a blank slate and construct ideas by interpreting our surrounding world. We depicted the creative process as it often unfolds: unpredictably." The story of searching for ideas is told in stages, beginning at Square One and ending in Utopia. In each photo, a blank rectangle represents the elusive idea (and reminds the reader of the paper). "The resulting piece—targeted at designers—positions Appleton Papers Utopia as the only constant in the organic process of finding a great idea: a tabula rasa that dares one to begin. The main character is a painter from Brooklyn. We painted his studio wall light blue for the cover photo. He left it that way. The 'Osmosis' shot was taken at the New York Metropolitan Museum of Art; it took a long time to find an empty room. The transvestites in 'Reevaluation' are Cyndi Lauper's backup singers."

STUDIO: João Machado Design Lda., Porto, Portugal **ART DIRECTOR:** João Machado **DESIGNER:** João Machado **ILLUSTRATOR:** João Machado **PHOTOGRAPHER:** Luis Ferreira Alves **CLIENT:** Town Council of Guimarães, Portugal **SOFTWARE:** QuarkXPress, Adobe Photoshop **PAPER:** Marcata, Nettuno, Keaycolour **COLORS:** 4, process **PAGES:** 72 **SIZE:** 14 15/16" x 9 1/2" (37.9cm x 24.1cm) (book); 15" x 9 11/16" (38.1cm x 24.7cm) (folder, closed) **TYPEFACES:** Gamada, Cochin **INSPIRATION:** "The medieval atmosphere of the city," says designer João Machado. Large photographs and textured paper showcase the wood, stone, brick and tile in the city's architecture. **CONCEPT:** The book outlines strategic goals for the city of Guimarães, which had just been named a World Heritage City for historically significant, and still vital, urban spaces. The book explains the history and future goals for the town in both English and Portuguese, kept equally distinct and readable by printing the two texts in parallel columns, one printed in black and one in gray. The pages brim with color photographs in many shapes and sizes, "revealing the architectural and urban heritage in the culture of Guimarães." **SPECIAL FOLDS OR FEATURES:** The cover is a large folder, which holds both the book and two topographical maps.

STUDIO: The Designers Republic, Sheffield, U.K. **ART DIRECTOR/DESIGNER:** The Designers Republic **ILLUSTRATOR:** The Designers Republic **PHOTOGRAPHERS:** Lord Peter Ashworth (printed by Brian Dowling at BDI London); Jeremy Chaplin (printed by LTI, London); Kevin Davies; The Designers Republic **CLIENT/PRODUCT:** Murray & Vern/fetish clubwear and fashion **SOFTWARE:** Macromedia FreeHand, Adobe Photoshop **COLORS:** 4, process plus 1, match metallic and a double pass of 1, match (cover); 1, match plus spot gloss varnish (inside cover); 4, process plus spot varnish (interior pages) **PAGES:** 32 **SIZE:** 10⅞" x 6¾" (27.5cm x 17.2cm) **PRINT RUN:** 5,000 **TYPEFACES:** Bell Gothic Black, DR TYP01 FG Square-ular (DR Font)
CONCEPT: "The concept for the design for this piece was: The Designers Republic vs. Murray & Vern, and, ultimately the entire fashion world," says designer Ian Anderson. Provocative photography, deconstructed and mock-technical artwork, and sparse but tart copy are designed to appeal to a narrow and defined audience.
SPECIAL PRODUCTION TECHNIQUES: "Complete Knowledge of Print."

STUDIO: Eg.G, Sheffield, U.K. **ART DIRECTOR:** Dom Raban **DESIGNER:** Dom Raban **WRITER:** Keith Jaffrate **PHOTOGRAPHER:** Paula Summerley **CLIENT/SERVICE:** Photo 98/arts organization **SOFTWARE:** Adobe Photoshop, Adobe Illustrator **PAPER:** Silk (cover and text) **COLORS:** 4, process plus match metallic and seal varnish **PAGES:** 42, plus 8-page cover **SIZE:** 6⅞" x 3¼" (17.5cm x 8.2cm)(folded); 6⅞" x 62⅞" (17.5cm x 159.7cm)(unfolded) **PRINT RUN:** 500 **COST PER UNIT:** UK£11.50 **TYPEFACES:** Officina Sans, Officina Serif **CONCEPT:** "Photo 98 was a publicly funded body set up to commission a number of arts projects throughout the U.K. during 1998," says designer Dom Raban. "Body:Ink was one of these commissions. It is a collaboration between writer (Keith Jaffrate), dancer (Charlotte Vincent), photographer (Paula Summerley) and designer (ourselves), examining the relationship between writing, photography and movement. Photographs are hardly ever seen unaccompanied by text; the text influences the way an image is read, whilst the connection between photography and movement was established from the very beginning by pioneers like Eadweard Muybridge. Body:Ink's intent is to look at ways of re-presenting these disparate, yet interconnected, disciplines. "The format of the brochure itself (very long concertina-folded book) has resonance with durational dance performance, whilst the treatment of the text could in many ways be described as photographic. Text flows from one side of the page to the other, emphasizing the fluidity of the piece. The typographic contrast between small and large point sizes and serif and sans serif, sometimes within single words, also stresses the idea of movement." **SPECIAL FEATURES:** The 42-page, concertina fold booklet is made from three sections glued together. It has an 8-page, glued-on cover.

STUDIO: Miriello Grafico, Inc., San Diego **ART DIRECTORS:** Ron Miriello, Michelle Aranda, Terry Christensen **DESIGNERS:** Nick Abadilla, Michelle Aranda, Liz Bernal, Terry Christensen, Courtney Mayer, Ron Miriello, Maureen Wood **ILLUSTRATORS:** Nick Abadilla, Michelle Aranda, Liz Bernal, Terry Christensen, Courtney Mayer, Ron Miriello, Daniel Renner, Maureen Wood **PHOTOGRAPHER:** Paul Body **CLIENT:** Self **SOFTWARE:** Adobe Illustrator, Adobe Photoshop **PAPER:** Patina Cover **COLORS:** 4, process plus match metallic and varnish **PAGES:** 15 cards in a CD jewel case, with cardboard mailing box and printed label **SIZE:** 5 1/2" x 4 5/8" (13.8cm x 11.8cm) **PRINT RUN:** 2,000 **COST PER UNIT:** approx. US$4 **TYPEFACES:** Franklin Gothic, various **INSPIRATION:** "We wanted to create a piece that would be used and referred to all year long, and that would involve the entire staff in the design," says art director Ron Miriello. "We wanted people to look at an image for the entire month and discover things throughout the year." **CONCEPT:** "The concept came out of how, with a fresh eye and an open mind, there is creative inspiration all around us. The design was inspired by re-using press proofs, found objects, inspirations and abandoned creative from the previous year. Each staff member created a face image using their own year's collections. Clients saw reminders of the projects we'd done together during the past year. We wanted to expose another, more personal, side of ourselves and a fuller picture of our people." **SPECIAL COST-CUTTING TECHNIQUES:** "All components were printed on one sheet, including the cover label. Very easy to assemble."

STUDIO: Power of Beauty Co., Ltd., Tokyo, Japan **ART DIRECTOR:** MIC*ITAYA **DESIGN:** MIC*ITAYA, Tabou (POB Design Division) **DESIGNERS:** Tomoko Nakabayashi, Hiroko Kawamura, Bou Ishimatsu **ILLUSTRATOR:** MIC*ITAYA **PHOTOGRAPHERS:** MIC*ITAYA, Takeo Ogiso, Jiro Fukasawa, AKI **CLIENT:** Korinsha Press **SIZE:** 5⅞" x 4½" (15cm x 11.3cm) **PRINT RUN:** 5,000 **TYPEFACES:** Calligraphic Japanese script, Bureau (both by MIC*ITAYA) **INSPIRATION:** "Books of travels and passports," says MIC*ITAYA. Both seemed perfect jumping-off points for a tiny exhibition catalog. A mock-suede cover showcases MIC*ITAYA's distinct style, which combines Japanese and Western elements. Inside, full-color illustrations on glossy paper provide an intriguing mix of art and travelogue. **SPECIAL PRODUCTION TECHNIQUES:** Hot-stamped cover.

STUDIO: Sibley Peteet Design, Dallas, TX **ART DIRECTOR/DESIGNER:** David Beck **ILLUSTRATORS:** various **PHOTOGRAPHERS:** various **COPYWRITER:** Margie Bowles **CLIENT/SERVICE:** The Image Bank/stock photography, illustration and film **SOFTWARE:** QuarkXPress, Adobe Illustrator **COLORS:** 4, process plus 2, match **PAGES:** 24 **SIZE:** 12" x 8⅛" (30.5cm x 20.7cm) **PRINT RUN:** 10,000 (first run) **COST PER UNIT:** US$0.85 **TYPEFACES:** various, including Bodoni, Futura, Bernhard Modern **CONCEPT:** "The Image Bank wanted to do a piece showing innovative use of their stock photography and illustration—not a 'hard sell' piece," says designer David Beck. "Using some unexpected juxtapositions, we helped show some of the depth and breadth of their vast collection of images." **SPECIAL PRODUCTION TECHNIQUES:** Because Image Bank is an international company, copies of the book needed to be printed in six languages. "We let this influence our layout by placing all of the copy on uncoated short sheets that would run through the book," Beck explains. "This way print production would be easier, because only that uncoated press form would have to be altered to accommodate the type changes. The majority of the book—with all the color images—would be universal to all versions. All this set up a nice contrast between the different paper stocks and different image styles." **SPECIAL FOLDS OR FEATURES:** Various graphic die-cuts, including a face in profile and a movie ticket, enhance the concept. The back cover folds in to reveal three perforated, full-color postcards. **SPECIAL COST-CUTTING TECHNIQUES:** "We were able to print this in Hong Kong, where The Image Bank prints its big catalogs, so it cost about one-third of what it would have here."

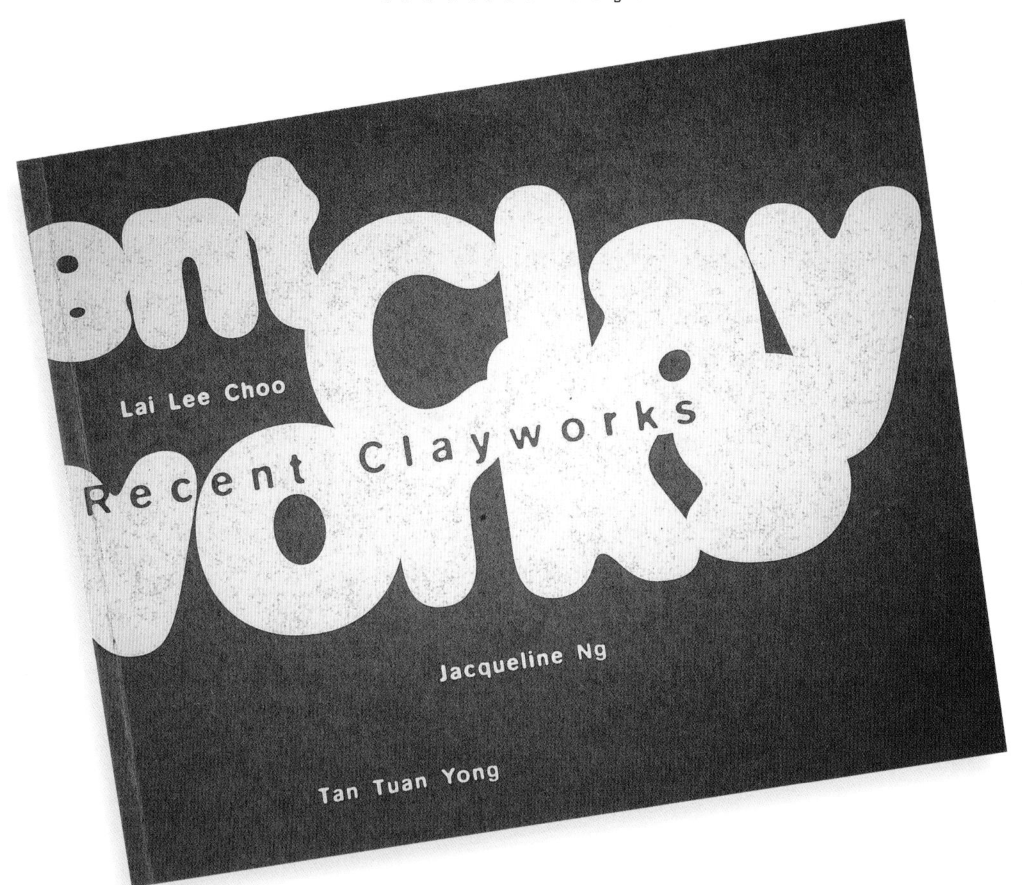

STUDIO: Epigram Pte Ltd., Singapore **ART DIRECTOR:** Edmund Wee **DESIGNER:** Paul van der Veer **PHOTOGRAPHERS:** Henry Foong (clayworks), Beh Kay Yi (portraits) **CLIENTS/SERVICE:** Lai Lee Choo, Ng Eng Teck, Tan Tuan Yong/artists **SOFTWARE:** QuarkXPress **PAPER:** Reprise 100% Recycled-Green (cover), Conservation-Wove (text) **COLORS:** 4, process **PAGES:** 24 plus cover **SIZE:** 8" x 10" (20.3cm x 25.4cm) **PRINT RUN:** 1,000 **TYPEFACE:** Blur **CONCEPT:** The diverse work of three artists is presented in this unusual catalog, which combines color photographs with hidden black-and-white sketches. To view the sketches, the recipient has to cut the pages or peer through the folds. **SPECIAL PRODUCTION TECHNIQUES:** The "double cover" brochure was printed in black on one side and full color on the other, scored and folded with the one-color printing inside, then perfect bound on the open edge. The result is a booklet of folded pages. The cover is screen-printed.

your image. It's how the world sees you. You need compelling solutions. Engaging design.
613.789.0244
storm. Design communications in a changing environment.

STUDIO: Storm Visual Communications Inc., Ottawa, Ontario, Canada **ART DIRECTOR/DESIGNER:** Robert Smith **PHOTOGRAPHER:** Headlight Innovative Imagery **PRINTER:** The Lowe-Martin Group **CLIENT:** Self **SOFTWARE:** QuarkXPress, Adobe Photoshop **PAPER:** Potlatch McCoy Gloss **COLORS:** 2, match blacks plus 1, match metallic; 2 varnishes **PAGES:** 10 **SIZE:** 8" x 9" (20.3cm x 23cm) **PRINT RUN:** 500 **COST PER UNIT:** Can$14 **TYPEFACE:** Trade Gothic **INSPIRATION:** "I wanted to create a visual contrast between the company name and the design execution," says designer Robert Smith. "Sparse type, abundant white space and heavy ink combine to create a pace that is engaging for the reader. The payoff is a bright, full-color photo at the end, showing a positive outcome." **CONCEPT:** "To use a storm as a metaphor to describe communications in today's world. The use of words, such as 'anticipate' and 'react,' as visual punctuation allowed us to tie the visual elements with the written concept. We wanted it to be light on text, yet direct and memorable. The use of Trade Gothic gives the piece a timeless aesthetic. The typeface doesn't conform to current design trends and will therefore give the piece more longevity." **SPECIAL PRODUCTION TECHNIQUE:** "The photos are tritones, using two blacks with a metallic ink that was dry-trapped. Two off-line varnishes were used to enhance the photos, and were also dry-trapped. Eyelets were used for binding to enhance the unique feel." **SPECIAL FEATURES:** "We folded the inside pages, which allowed us to print on one side of the sheet, reducing showthrough and making the brochure thicker and more substantial."

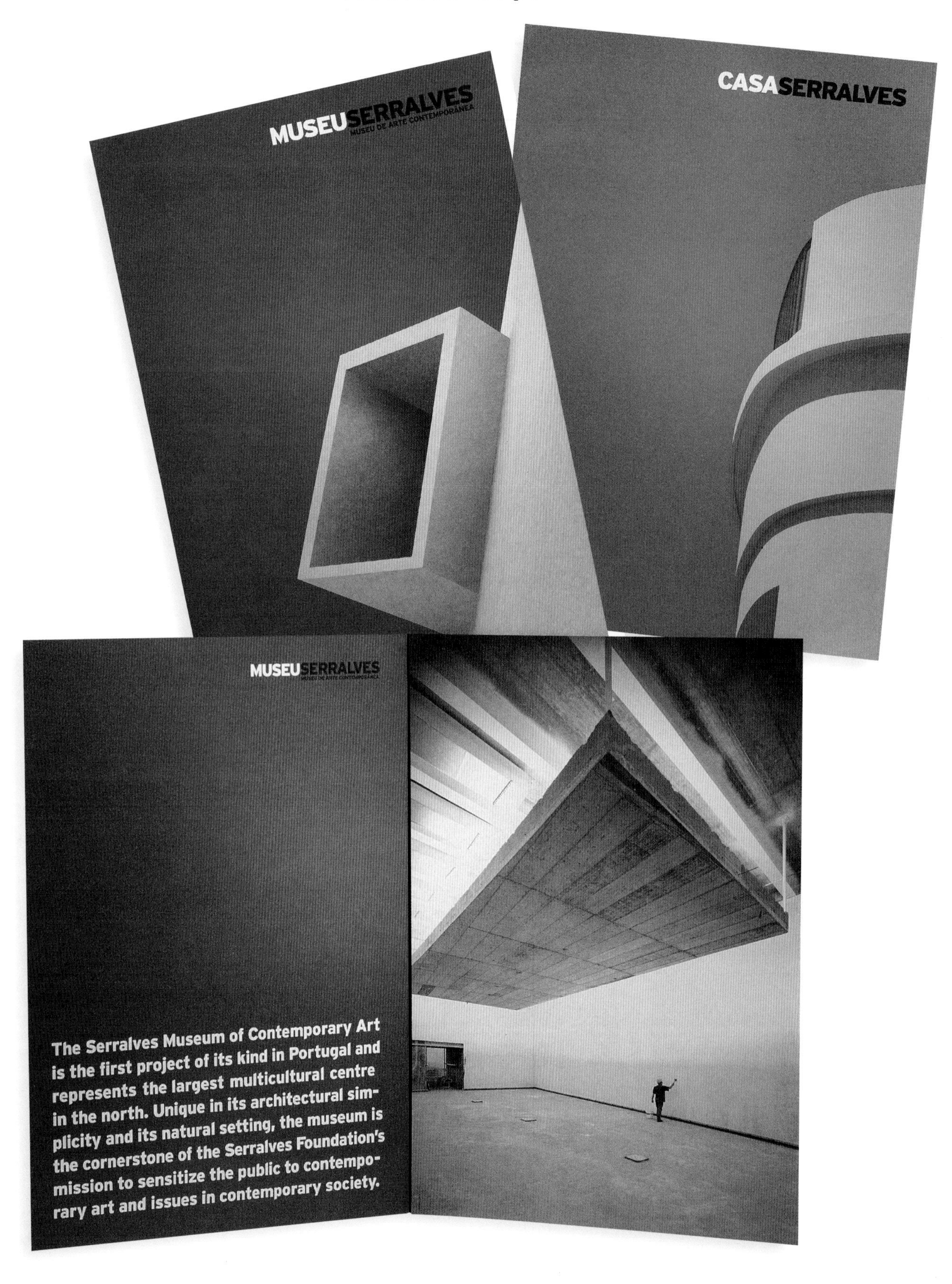

STUDIO: Future Brand (formerly Diefenbach Elkins Davies Baron), London, U.K. **ART DIRECTOR:** Wladimir Marnich **DESIGNERS:** Wladimir Marnich, Sotos Georgialli **PHOTOGRAPHERS:** James Cant, Luis Ferreira Alves **CLIENT:** Museu de Serralves **SOFTWARE:** QuarkXPress **PAPER:** Munken Pure **COLORS:** 4, process plus 1, match **PAGES:** 6 **SIZE:** 16½" x 11¹¹⁄₁₆" (42cm x 29.7cm) **PRINT RUN:** 2,000 (each) **TYPEFACES:** Interstate Black, Trade Gothic **CONCEPT:** The idea behind this series of four brochures, says designer Wladimir Marnich, was to convey a sense of modernity through scale. "To show sections of the buildings to suggest the scale and minimal approach of the architecture became a logical solution, considering that two of the three buildings shown weren't finished," he explains. "Retouching turned red brick walls into smooth white concrete. We used a large-format brochure to create a sense of scale and modernity that we could not achieve through the use of images."

CASASERRALVES

The Casa Serralves, located in the heart of Oporto on an 18 hectare park, is the seat of the Serralves Foundation and an indispensable part of the Serralves Museum of Contemporary Art. Finished in 1940, the Serralves mansion is a unique example of work of some of the leading architects and designers of the 1920s and 1930s, including Siclis, Lalique and Ruhlmann. Today, it houses temporary collections of contemporary artists and permanent works of the museum.

PARQUESERRALVES

AUDITÓRIOSERRALVES

AUDITÓRIOSERRALVES

The Serralves Auditorium, an integral part of the Serralves Museum of Contemporary Art, provides a new and exciting venue for the performing arts, film, conferences and workshops. Located in the heart of an 18 hectare park, the Auditorium brings together in one intimate state-of-the-art space the necessary elements to complement the activities of the Museum and the Serralves Park and provide a varied programme of events for the public.

STUDIO: Chantry/Sheehan, Seattle, WA **ART DIRECTOR:** Art Chantry **DESIGNER:** Art Chantry **PHOTOGRAPHERS:** Marty Sohl, Marit Brook-Kothlow, David Loseno, Aengus McMahon, Kim Zumwalt, Christine Alicino, Jim Dennis **CLIENT/SERVICE:** Nemzoff/Roth Touring Artists/arts management **SOFTWARE:** none **PAPER:** Newsprint **COLORS:** 3, match **PAGES:** 8 **SIZE:** 24" x 18" (61cm x 45.7cm) **PRINT RUN:** 1,000 **COST PER UNIT:** US$0.25 **TYPEFACE:** Futura Bold Condensed (Paul Rennard) **INSPIRATION:** "An old promo item by the late Wes Anderson." **CONCEPT:** Folded in fours, the piece looks like an unassuming mailer. Unfolded, it becomes a book of three-color posters for different arts projects and performances. The distinctive grainy images make ink-soaking paper and less-than-precise printing a virtue. They were produced, Chantry says, "by photocopying them until they rotted apart." **SPECIAL COST-CUTTING TECHNIQUE:** "Nonheat-set offset newspaper web printing," says designer Art Chantry, "is CHEAP!"

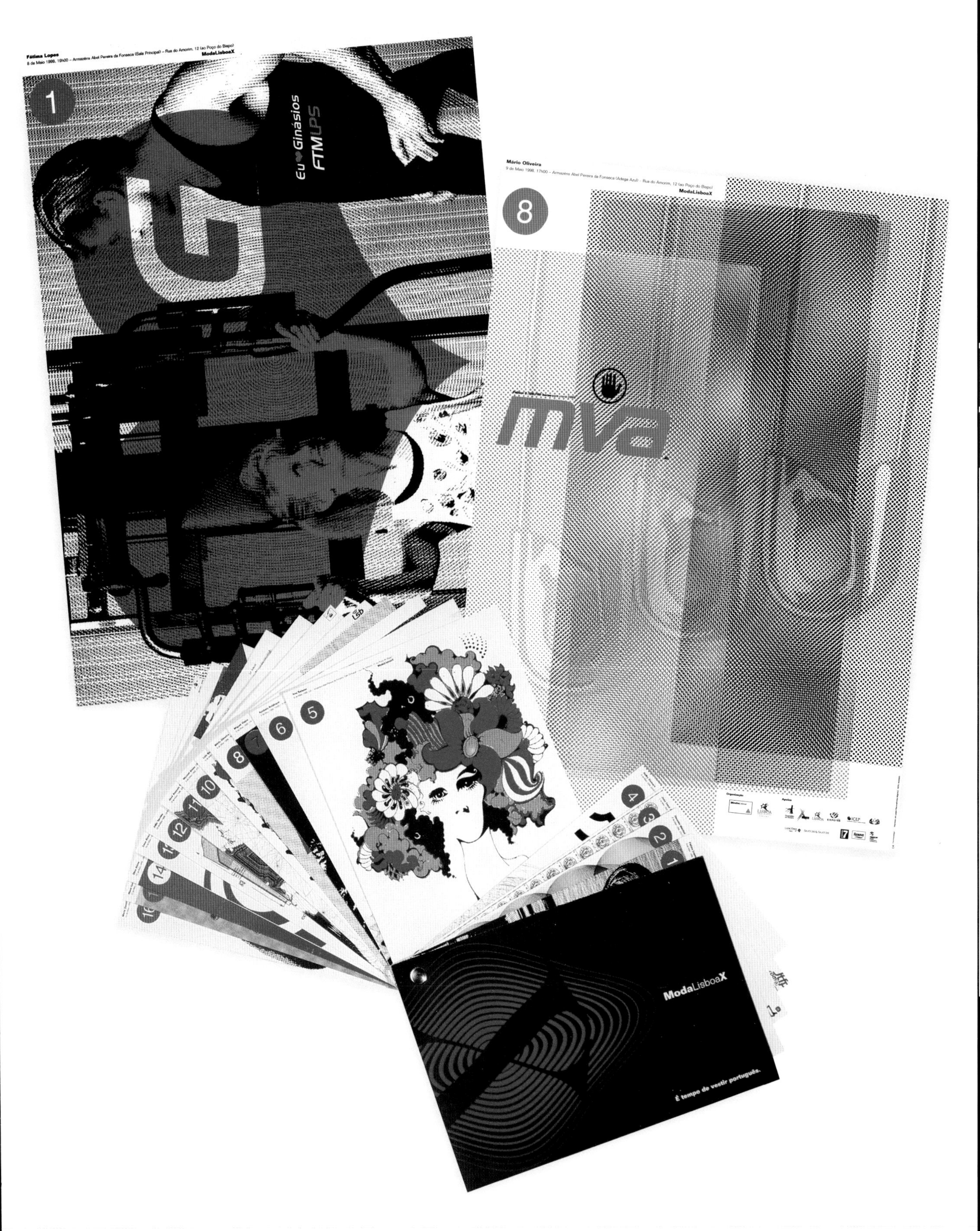

STUDIO: Ricardo Mealha, Atelier de Design, Lda., Lisbon, Portugal **ART DIRECTOR/DESIGNER:** Ricardo Mealha **CLIENT:** Associação Moda Lisboa **SOFTWARE:** Macromedia FreeHand, Adobe Streamline **COLORS:** 2, match **PAGES:** 15 (VIP invitation); 1 (regular invitation) **SIZE:** 3" x 4¼" (7.5cm x 10.7cm) (booklet); 23 ¼" x 16 ½" (59cm x 41.9cm) (posters) **PRINT RUN:** 1,500 (regular invitation); 800 (VIP invitation) **TYPEFACES:** Helvetica, Dingbats **INSPIRATION:** The eclectic taste and trends of the 1990s: technology, religion, retro chic and Asian influences. The look is a bit kitschy, with black and magenta silhouettes reminiscent of the 1980s mixed with cyber lettering.

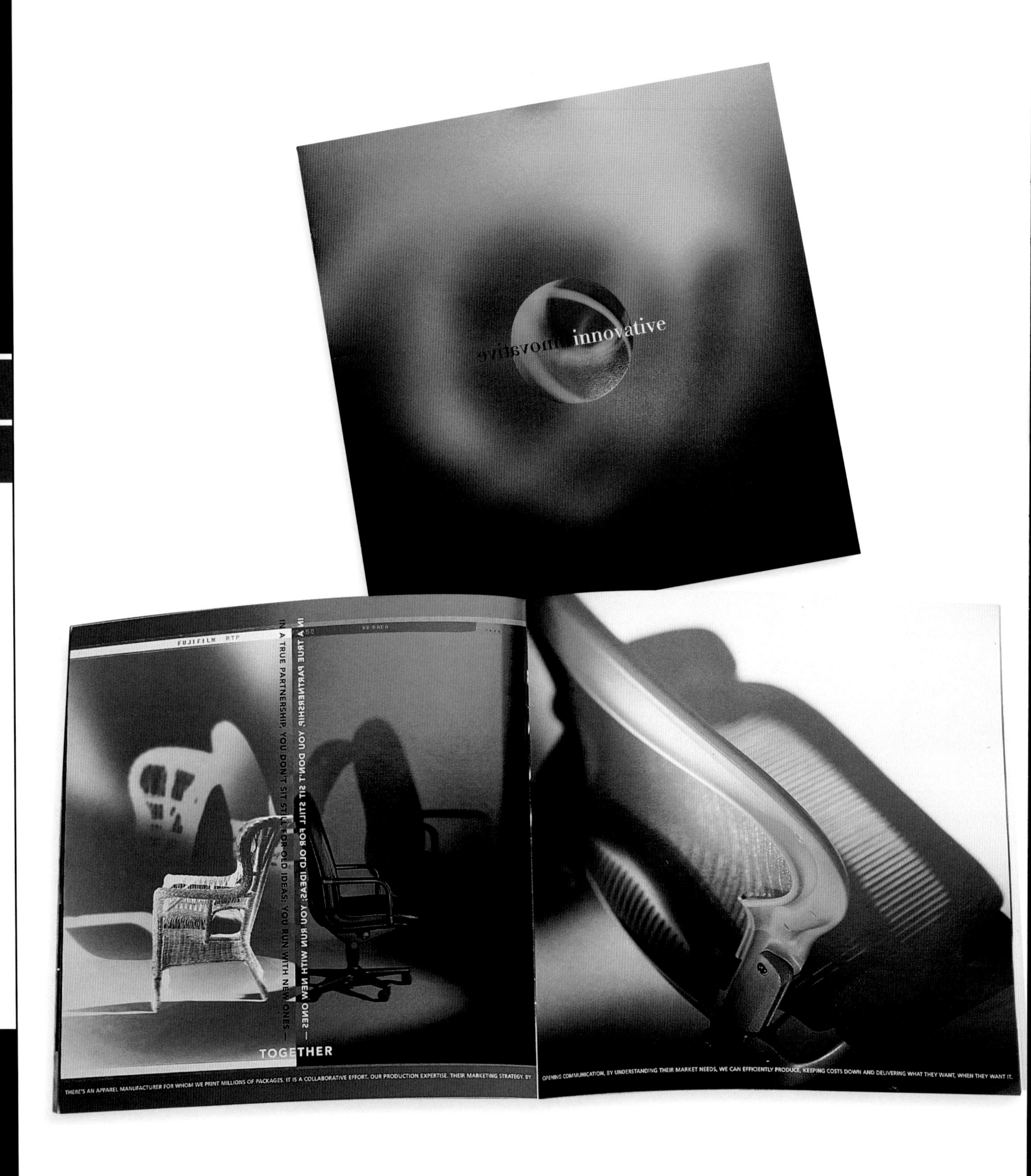

STUDIO: Wages Design, Inc., Atlanta, GA **ART DIRECTORS:** Bob Wages, Randall Allison **DESIGNER:** Randall Allison **ILLUSTRATOR:** Randall Allison **COPYWRITING:** Scott Suhr **PHOTOGRAPHER:** Jerry Burns **CLIENT/PRODUCT:** Cadmus Communications/printing **SOFTWARE:** QuarkXPress, Adobe Photoshop, Adobe Illustrator **PAPER:** Opus Gloss Cover (cover); Opus Web Gloss (text) **COLORS:** 4, process plus 3, match **PAGES:** 24 **SIZE:** 11" x 11" (28cm x 28cm) **TYPEFACES:** Futura, Frutiger **INSPIRATION:** "Innovation." **CONCEPT:** "Each spread featured the contrast of great products and innovations that made the products even better," says designer Randall Allison. "These innovations were then related to Cadmus and the innovative ideas and methods they provide their customers." **SPECIAL PRODUCTION TECHNIQUE:** On several spreads, three fluorescent inks were substituted for cyan, magenta and yellow. Type was manipulated in Adobe Illustrator with KPT Vector effects.

STUDIO: Mortensen Design, Mountain View, CA **ART DIRECTOR:** Gordon Mortensen **DESIGNERS:** Gordon Mortensen, P.J. Nidecker **PHOTOGRAPHERS:** Pierre-Yves Goavec, Geoffrey Nelson (page 2) **CLIENT/SERVICE:** Identix Incorporated/fingerprint capture and verification technology **SOFTWARE:** QuarkXPress, Macromedia FreeHand **PAPER:** Utopia Silk Cover, Utopia Silk Book **COLORS:** 5, process plus varnish over 4, process plus varnish (cover); 7, match and process plus varnish (text) **PAGES:** 8 plus cover **SIZE:** 11½" x 8½" (29.3cm x 21.6cm) **PRINT RUN:** 27,000 **COST PER UNIT:** US$2.87 **TYPEFACES:** Futura (Adobe)(headlines), Times Roman (Adobe)(text) **INSPIRATION:** "The unique photographic style of photographer Pierre-Yves Goavec," says designer Gordon Mortensen. **CONCEPT:** Two custom photos illustrate Identix's two top product areas: biometric security, for commercial industry; and biometric imaging, for law enforcement. Both photos, together with the cover art, represent how fingerprints can be used to provide security and safety.

STUDIO: Louey/Rubino Design Group Inc., Santa Monica, CA **ART DIRECTOR:** Robert Louey **DESIGNER:** Robert Louey **ILLUSTRATOR:** David Lesh **WRITER:** Elisabeth Charney **CLIENT:** Cast Management Consultants, Inc. **SOFTWARE:** QuarkXPress **PAPER:** Mead Signature Dull **COLORS:** 4, process plus 1, match and varnish **PAGES:** 12 **SIZE:** 10½" x 7" (26.7cm x 17.8cm) **PRINT RUN:** 10,000 **TYPEFACE:** Trade Gothic Condensed **INSPIRATION:** "Simplicity." **CONCEPT:** According to designer Robert Louey, the piece used stock illustrations and spare type to convey the idea of "intelligent problem solving in relation to 'true to life' conditions of modern business." The short, readable text explains the company's services in detail. One each text page, one word in extra-small type, printed in red ink, gives a "snapshot" of the firm's promises to its clients. **SPECIAL PRODUCTION TECHNIQUES:** The company name is embossed on the cover. **SPECIAL COST-CUTTING TECHNIQUES:** Use of stock illustrations.

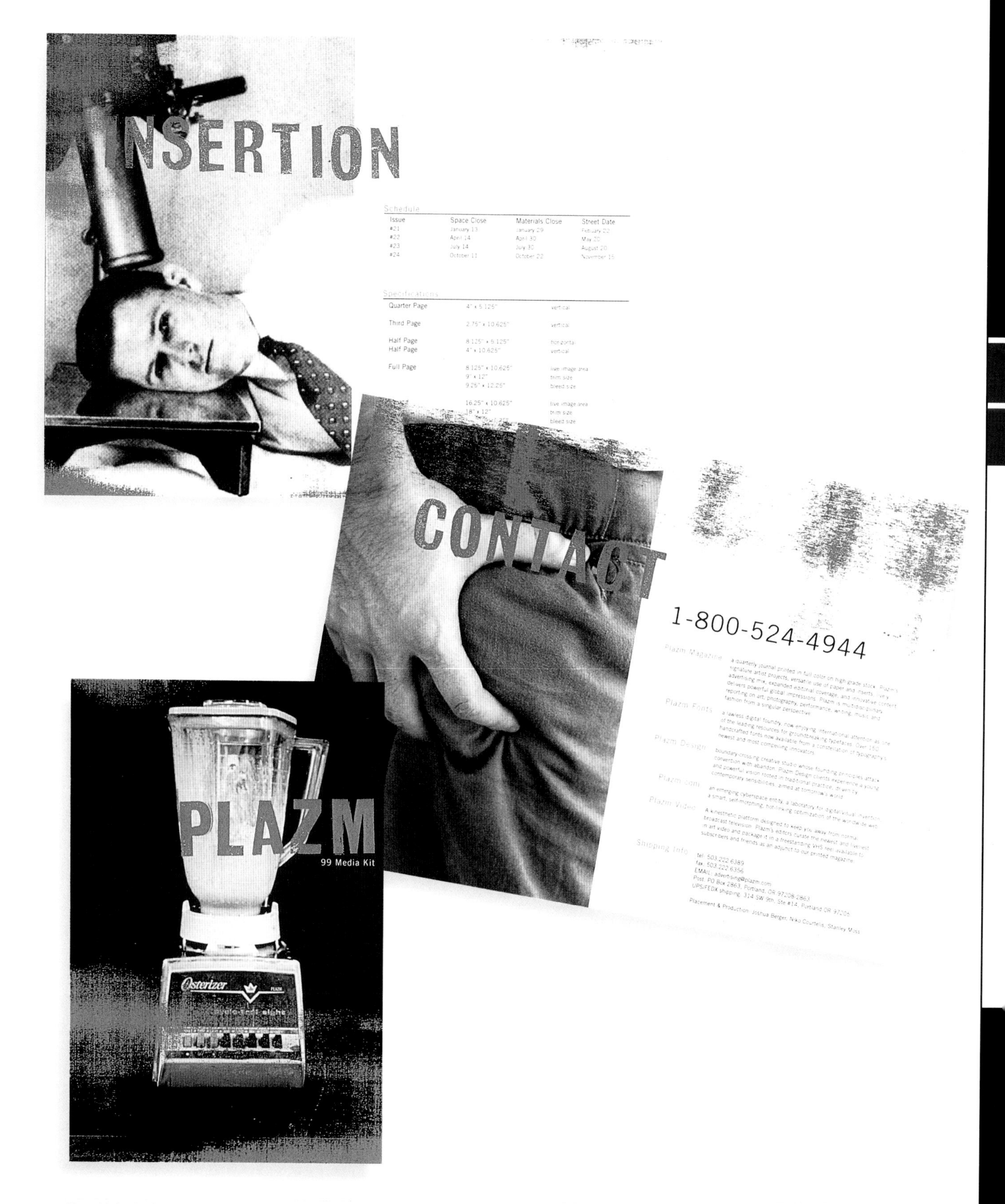

STUDIO: Plazm Media, Portland, OR **ART DIRECTORS:** Joshua Berger, Niko Courtelis, Pete McCracken **DESIGNERS:** Niko Courtelis, Dylan Nelson **PHOTOGRAPHERS:** Sumaya Agha, Dan Garland **CLIENT:** Plazm Magazine **SOFTWARE:** Adobe Photoshop, QuarkXPress **PAPER:** Newsprint **COLORS:** 2, match **PAGES:** 24 **SIZE:** 7 ½" x 11" (19cm x 27.9cm) **PRINT RUN:** 5,000 **COST PER UNIT:** US$0.30 **TYPEFACE:** News Gothic **INSPIRATION:** "Most media kits are really dry," says art director Joshua Berger. "Plazm Magazine is exactly the opposite of really dry. We wanted to create a media kit which finally told the truth about Plazm!" **CONCEPT:** "Be ourselves. Represent the magazine. Enough with the sales pitch, let's try honesty." **SPECIAL TYPE TECHNIQUES:** "Photocopy. Photocopy. Photocopy." **SPECIAL PRODUCTION TECHNIQUES:** "Lowest grade paper and printing we could find." **SPECIAL FEATURES:** "Two staples and the truth!"

STUDIO: Power of Beauty Co., Ltd., Tokyo, Japan **ART DIRECTOR:** MIC*ITAYA **DESIGN:** MIC*ITAYA, Tabou (POB Design Division) **DESIGNERS:** Noriyuki Yakota and Bou Ishimatsu, Tabou; Sanemasa Mushakoji, Cherubim **ILLUSTRATOR:** MIC*ITAYA **PHOTOGRAPHERS:** MIC*ITAYA, Takeo Ogiso, Jiro Fukasawa, Mitsuo Shindo, AKI, Prime Factor **CLIENT:** Korinsha Press **SIZE:** 8" x 6" (20.5cm x 15cm) **PRINT RUN:** 3,000 **TYPEFACES:** PIM, Bureau (both by MIC*ITAYA) **INSPIRATION:** "Our earth is but a small part of the universe," says MIC*ITAYA, who opened the book with this epigram. **CONCEPT:** "This book is a report on our activities, such as exhibitions, through 1996 and 1997. The paper book cover can also be used, unfolded, for PR posters. This reflects the coexistence of artistic and realistic expression in our design, and also leads to the basic philosophy of MIC*ITAYA and its design activities." **SPECIAL PRODUCTION TECHNIQUES:** The cover illustration is hot-stamped on mock-suede paper. Three bookmarks are tipped in, and the credit pages are printed in metallic silver for added impact. The paper stock is particularly thick, for a distinct feel, and four-color process sections alternate with various two-color sections.

Margaret Howell
The J. Peterman Company
123
150
151

STUDIO: Weaver Design, Birmingham, AL **DESIGNER:** Marie Weaver **PHOTOGRAPHERS:** Hugh Hunter, Alan Hunter **COPYWRITER:** Tom Wofford **CLIENT/SERVICE:** hunterphotography/still photos and video **SOFTWARE:** QuarkXPress, Adobe Illustrator, Adobe Photoshop **PAPER:** S.D. Warren LOE Gloss Cover **COLORS:** 4, process plus dull varnish **PAGES:** 14 panels **SIZE:** 6" x 4⅛" (15.2cm x 10.2cm)(folded); 6" x 28½" (15.2cm x 72.3cm)(unfolded) **PRINT RUN:** 3,500 **COST PER UNIT:** US$0.38 **TYPEFACES:** Matrix (Emigre), Schmutz Cleaned (Image Club) **INSPIRATION:** "The more concrete inspiration was the photography and videography of Hugh and Alan Hunter, their personalities and contemporary culture," says designer Marie Weaver. "One of the brothers is low-key and the other is, well, lively. So each brother has a side of the brochure: two men, two creative businesses, but one basic operation because they work together on many projects." **CONCEPT:** The strategic goals were announcing Hunter Films, connecting it to the longstanding business of Hunter Photography and allowing each its own identity. "We intended to create new business by showing the audience samples of excellent past work," Weaver says. "But we all know that hiring creatives has a lot to do with who you want to hang out with for a day's shoot. Therefore, it was important to imply something about the personalities of Hugh and Alan. The copywriter, Tom Wofford, made the tone kind of hip, playful and a little daring—because everybody knows that artists are like that—but not too intimidating, because a lot of the Hunters' business comes from corporations." **SPECIAL PRODUCTION TECHNIQUES:** Each end of the brochure is die-cut. Dull varnish over gloss paper gives better contrast than printing gloss varnish over matte paper. **SPECIAL FOLDS OR FEATURES:** The accordion-folded brochure was mailed in a UV envelope, enticing recipients with color. **SPECIAL COST-CUTTING TECHNIQUES:** The designer traded design work for photography and video editing.

STUDIO: Campbell Fisher Ditko Design, Phoenix, AZ **ART DIRECTOR:** Steve Ditko **DESIGNER:** Steve Ditko **PHOTOGRAPHER:** Bruce Racine **CLIENT/SERVICE:** Racine Photo Arts/photography **SOFTWARE:** Adobe Illustrator **PAPER:** Chipboard, Springhill Tag UV **COLORS:** 4, process **PAGES:** 16 **SIZE:** 5½" x 5½" (13.9cm x 13.9cm) **PRINT RUN:** 1,000 **COST PER UNIT:** US$1 **TYPEFACE:** Schmutz Corroded (Image Club) **INSPIRATION:** Playing cards and collectible cards. **CONCEPT:** "Fortune cookie sayings combined with the photographer's images," says the designer. **SPECIAL FEATURES:** A die-cut holds the rubber binding gasket. Uncoated paper gives the printed photos a distinct look. **SPECIAL COST-CUTTING TECHNIQUES:** "We found gaskets at Home Depot for fifty-eight cents each, and bought them wholesale from the manufacturer for six cents each."

STUDIO: Ricardo Mealha, Atelier de Design, Lda., Lisbon, Portugal **ART DIRECTOR:** Ricardo Mealha **DESIGNER:** Carlos Rei **SOFTWARE:** Macromedia FreeHand, QuarkXPress, Adobe Photoshop **COLORS:** 4, process **SIZE:** 9⅞" x 9" (25cm x 23cm)(folded); 9⅞" x 36" (25cm x 91.4cm)(unfolded) **PRINT RUN:** 150,000 **TYPEFACES:** Beta Sans, Beta Semi, Alien Grey **CONCEPT:** "To establish and show the entire activities calendar for the two-month festival in the clearest and most linear way possible," say the designers. "That's the reason for the piece's shape, with days on the horizontal. We used color to mark the change from the first to the second month." **SPECIAL TYPE TECHNIQUE:** "Alien Grey is used only as a decorative element. It does not present any new information, it just repeats information given with the 'reading font.'"

STUDIO: Ricardo Mealha, Atelier de Design, Lda., Lisbon, Portugal **ART DIRECTOR:** Ricardo Mealha **DESIGNER:** Ana Margarida Cunha **SOFTWARE:** Macromedia FreeHand, Infini-D, Adobe Photoshop **COLORS:** 4, process plus 2, match **SIZE:** 11$^{11}/_{16}$" x 8¼" (29.7cm x 21cm) (folded) **PRINT RUN:** 1,000 **TYPEFACES:** Serpentine, Proton, Frutiger **CONCEPT:** "The graphic aspect is to illustrate that year's very futuristic trend. Three-dimensional illustrations and Photoshop images inside 3-D images create the look. The brochure is simultaneously functional and trendy."

Quit Talking To Me • 1997

23 x 42 inches, mixed media on silk screen frame.

FourPlay • 1997

6.25 x 8.25 inches, mixed media on cardboard.

Jack-O-Hearts • 1997

5.5 x 6.5 inches, mixed media on cardboard.

STUDIO: Mark Allen Design, Venice, CA **ART DIRECTOR/DESIGNER:** Mark Allen **ARTIST:** Mark Allen **CLIENT:** Self **SOFTWARE:** Adobe Photoshop, QuarkXPress, Fontographer **PAPER:** Great White Inkjet, 3M Transparency Film **COLORS:** 4, digital printout **PAGES:** 44 **SIZE:** 5⅝" x 4¼" (14.2cm x 10.8cm) **PRINT RUN:** as needed **COST PER UNIT:** approx. US$13.10 **TYPEFACES:** Meridien, Shelly Allegro, Nellakram, Fandango, Democratica, Poplar, Helvetica **INSPIRATION:** Mark Allen, an artist, says, "In order to have your artwork considered by an art gallery, you must first go through the ritual of shooting slides, then compiling a bunch of made-up crap about yourself and tossing this thing in the mail and hoping. I thought, 'There has to be a better way! What if all this information was presented beautifully in a book? That should get their attention.' So I created this book featuring my fine art assemblages and collages." **CONCEPT:** "I got tired of forever waiting for a publisher to come along and offer to print up a beautifully bound book on my art. So I decided to produce it in-house on my trusty-krusty Epson color printer; I could experiment with different types of paper to add to the tactile quality of the book. Printing on the transparency film added a nice additional dimension to the pages printed on paper. Keeping the size small makes it easy to mail out to prospective art buyers and art dealers. Getting them to return the books is a different story." **SPECIAL TYPE TECHNIQUES:** "A combination of an understated classic book layout with a hint of experimental type treatments in the introduction to add some excrement (I mean excitement) to the design without overpowering the artwork," says Allen. "The font used on the cover, Nellakram (Mark Allen backwards), was created by hand and scanned into Fontographer and cleaned up."

STUDIO: Volker Mueller Grafik Design, Koenigsbach-Stein, Germany **ART DIRECTOR:** Volker Mueller Grafik Design **DESIGNER:** Volker Mueller Grafik Design **ILLUSTRATOR:** Sabine Kussmaul **CLIENT/SERVICE:** Sabine Kussmaul/illustration **SOFTWARE:** QuarkXPress, Adobe Photoshop **PAPER:** Siriocolor Red Lampone (jacket and foreword); Siriocolor Nero (cover); MunkenPure Wood-free White (interior) **COLORS:** 4-color Euroskala **PAGES:** 16 **SIZE:** 8 7/8" x 6 1/2" (22.5cm x 16.6cm) **COST PER UNIT:** 3,40 DM **TYPEFACES:** Impact (Geoffrey Lee), Letter Gothic RG (Roger Robertson) **INSPIRATION:** "To create a unifying whole out of a large collection of illustrations with different themes," says designer Volker Mueller. "The idea was not to compose a picture book or compile a portfolio. Instead, the illustrator was asked to compose a text that would move the piece to a different level. Together with this text, the illustrations suddenly had a new meaning and created a story in their own right." **CONCEPT:** "Like the text, which takes a new spin from one page to the next, the layout of each page changes. The size of the illustrations varies, the pictures 'leap' across the pages as if by chance, and the type moves in the same way. Sabine Kussmaul is currently living in England, and her text incorporates both English and German. The two languages meet in a contrasting wave, which the font size reflects in its dramatic ebb and flow. The paper for the inside pages has a natural feel, rather like handmade paper, matching the natural cardboards that the illustrator often uses. The compact format and modest cover design provide a contrast to the dramatic interior."

We all know not to judge a book by its cover, but if everyone followed that advice, no one would have a career in book jacket or package design. Good packaging can enhance what's inside it, building expectations by either hiding or revealing its contents.

[packaging]

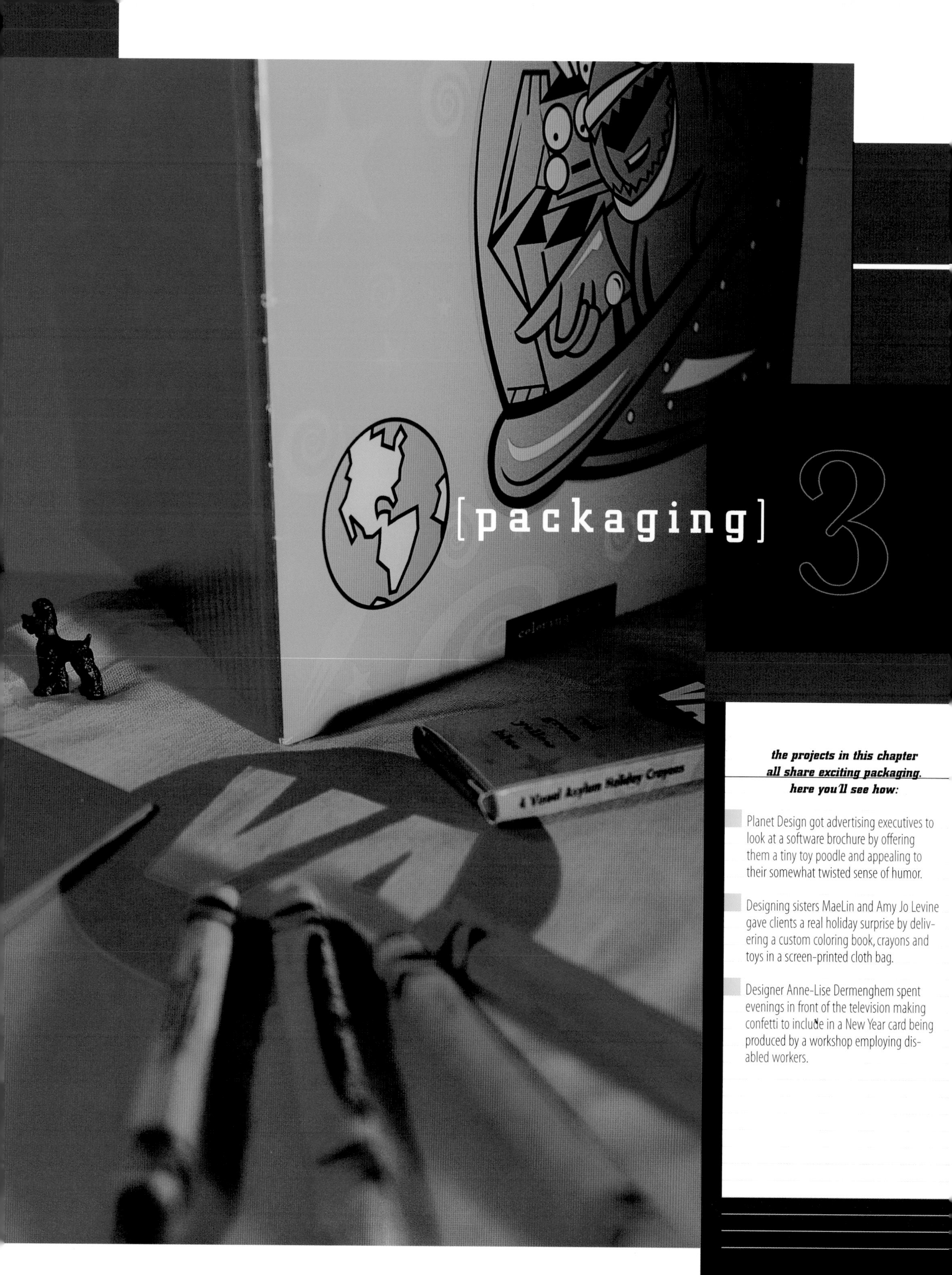

[packaging] 3

the projects in this chapter all share exciting packaging. here you'll see how:

- Planet Design got advertising executives to look at a software brochure by offering them a tiny toy poodle and appealing to their somewhat twisted sense of humor.
- Designing sisters MaeLin and Amy Jo Levine gave clients a real holiday surprise by delivering a custom coloring book, crayons and toys in a screen-printed cloth bag.
- Designer Anne-Lise Dermenghem spent evenings in front of the television making confetti to include in a New Year card being produced by a workshop employing disabled workers.

STUDIO: Ricardo Mealha, Atelier de Design, Lda., Lisbon, Portugal **ART DIRECTOR:** Ricardo Mealha **DESIGNER:** Ana Margarida Cunha **CLIENT/SERVICE:** Lux/nightclub **SOFTWARE:** Macromedia FreeHand, Adobe Photoshop **COLORS:** 4, process plus 1, match **SIZE:** 5 3/4" x 8 1/8" (14.7cm x 20.7cm)(package); 4 5/8" x 6 7/8" (11.7cm x 17.5cm)(cards) **PRINT RUN:** 5,000 **CONCEPT:** "The intention was, for the opening of a new club in Lisbon, to offer a souvenir object that has a relationship to the architecture," says art director Ricardo Mealha. "Like the building, it's a white object filled with colorful images. Surprise was also an important factor for the design of the piece." **SPECIAL FEATURES:** The club's name is molded into the white plastic container. The colorful cards have rounded edges, like the box.

[What is Curium?]
[creation is constant mutation]
In order for something to evolve it needs
to adapt to a changing environment.
CURIUM DESIGN
83 Divisadero Street • San Francisco • CA 94117
Phone: [415] 255-1877 Fax: [415] 255-6833
E-Mail: curium@designlink.com
CmD BROCHURE Mac
CURIUM DESIGN

STUDIO: Curium Design, San Francisco, CA **ART DIRECTOR/DESIGNER:** Evan Sornstein **ILLUSTRATOR:** Curium Design **PHOTOGRAPHER:** Curium Design **CLIENT:** Self **SOFTWARE:** QuarkXPress, Adobe Photoshop, Macromedia FreeHand **PAPER:** Standard coated text **COLORS:** 4, process **PAGES:** 8 **SIZE:** 4¾" x 4¾" (12.1cm x 12.1cm) **PRINT RUN:** 2,500 **COST PER UNIT:** US$2.50 **TYPEFACES:** Box31 (Curium Design), Futura, Moonbase Alpha **INSPIRATION:** "Neville Brody, Designers Republic, and science textbooks." **CONCEPT:** "We wanted to have it come across as scientific, yet philosophical," says Curium Design. "The philosophy of science. We packaged it in a jewel case to market to entertainment companies." **SPECIAL FEATURES:** This multimedia presentation was designed to fit on one floppy disk. It was packaged in a compact disk jewel case with an eight-page, saddle-stitched print brochure. **SPECIAL COST-CUTTING TECHNIQUES:** Only one side of the printed sheet was four-color process; the other was black and white. The result is a booklet with alternating color and black-and-white pages.

STUDIO: Eg.G, Sheffield, U.K. **ART DIRECTOR/DESIGNER:** Dom Raban **PHOTOGRAPHER:** Hugo Glendinning **CLIENT/SERVICE:** Forced Entertainment/theater company **SOFTWARE:** Adobe Photoshop, Adobe Illustrator **PAPER:** Recyconomic Offset (brochure), Crackback (stickers) **COLORS:** 1, match (brochure); 4, process (stickers) **PAGES:** 12 plus sticker insert **SIZE:** 5⅞" x 4⅛" (14.8cm x 10.5cm) (booklet); 5⅞" x 4" (14.8cm x 10.1cm) (stickers) **PRINT RUN:** 10,000 **COST PER UNIT:** UK£0.40 **TYPEFACE:** Univers **CONCEPT:** "Forced Entertainment is an experimental theater company, formed in 1984, who have worked widely both in Europe and the States," says designer Dom Raban. "This piece was intended to showcase three of their major pieces from the last four years, as well as giving a background to the company. However, as it is with most arts-based companies, budget was a prime consideration. So we designed a single-color brochure where you add your own color (stickers)—interactive print, if you like!"

STUDIO: Infinite Studio, Savona, Italy **ART DIRECTOR/DESIGNER:** Fabio Berruti **PHOTOGRAPHER:** Fabio Berruti **CLIENT/SERVICE:** Self/graphic and photography design for the music business **SOFTWARE:** QuarkXPress, Adobe Photoshop, Macromedia FreeHand **PAPER:** Fedrigoni Savile Row Tweed blue (cover), Fedrigoni Arcoprint (interior), Fedrigoni GSK E.W. (vellum) **COLORS:** 4, process (interior); 1, match (cover); 2, match (vellum) **PAGES:** 10 **SIZE:** 7 7/8" x 11 13/16" (20cm x 30cm) **COST PER UNIT:** US$2.30 **TYPEFACES:** Univers, Flux **INSPIRATION:** "A simple message, like a telegraph received from the hands of your usual mailman. For bookbinding I used a shabby string with a plumb (typically used in mail packages in Italy). I was saying: 'It's only a momentary book of my work—my work grows day by day. This is NOW, it's NON-definitive, it's only a passage.' Just a message." **CONCEPT:** "First of all: the papers. Three different papers, three different colors, three different messages. Cover: rough, dark; an orange print on black for logo (and back for E-mail address). First page and next to last: semitransparent to introduce the work. Internal pages: white, clear; show example of works, awards and publications. This three-level idea (just three papers) was the starting point." **SPECIAL PRODUCTION TECHNIQUES:** Handmade bookbinding.

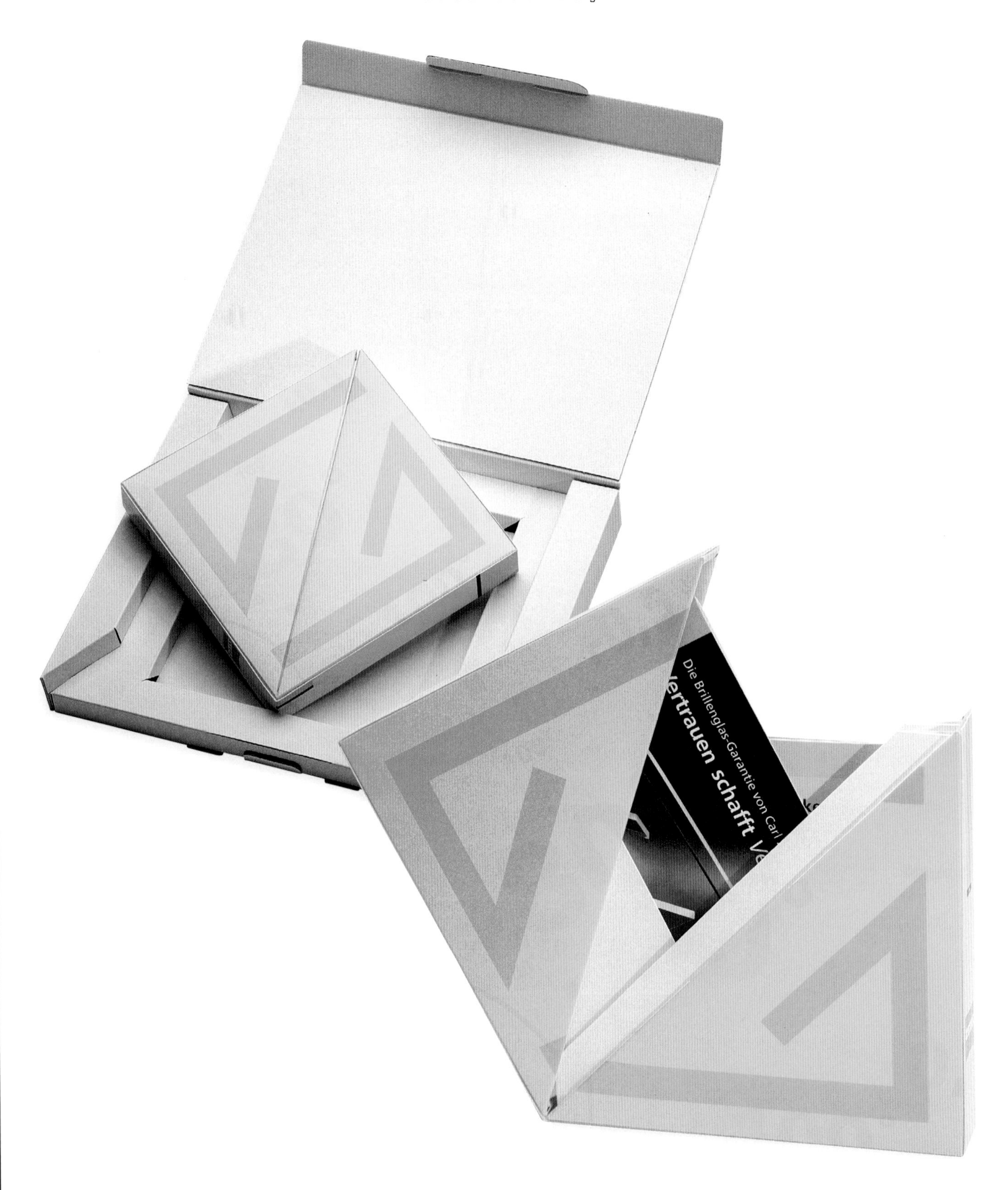

STUDIO: RTS Rieger Team Werbeagentur GmbH, Leinfelden-Echterdingen, Germany **ART DIRECTOR:** Otto Hedwig **CREATIVE DIRECTOR:** Boris Pollig **COPYWRITER:** Katja Miltner **PHOTOGRAPHER:** Michael Krasser **CLIENT/PRODUCT:** Carl Zeiss—Geschäftsbereich Augenoptik/lenses **SOFTWARE:** QuarkXPress **COLORS:** 4, process **SIZE:** 6" x 5⅞" (15.2cm x 14.9cm) (booklet); 6⅝" x 6¾" x 1⅝" (16.9cm x 17cm x 4.3cm) (hinged box, closed) **PRINT RUN:** 2,000 **TYPEFACES:** Frutiger Regular, Frutiger Bold **INSPIRATION:** "The Zeiss logo, which has a square format," says RTS spokesperson Jörg Dambacher. "We looked at a way to present the information in a cube. As lenses are a very technical product, technical elements such as dioptrical signs were printed on the box." **CONCEPT:** "Without a brand like Zeiss you could not think of glasses. And without opticians who work with Zeiss, you could not think of them either. Zeiss supports opticians with a number of advertising methods, to help them sell top-of-the-line lenses." Because opticians pay for Zeiss advertising, and also get advertising from Zeiss's competitors, the pieces must be as attractive and effective as possible. "So in the first place the concept was to clearly structure the advertising information for five product groups by creating individual packages that were constructed identically. Each package contains an advertisement, samples of flyers and letters for buyers, and a fax ordering form. Putting these items in one box helps the optician to have everything in one place."

Werbemitte
einer Br
en Sie für Ihre Aug

STUDIO: Alexander Isley Inc., Redding, CT **ART DIRECTOR:** Alexander Isley **DESIGNER:** Charles Robertson **ILLUSTRATORS:** Alexander Isley, Charles Robertson **PHOTOGRAPHER:** Richard Sexton **WRITERS:** Janet Abrams, Alan Kellogg Cowan, Alexander Isley **CLIENT:** The American Institute of Graphic Arts **SOFTWARE:** QuarkXPress, Adobe Illustrator, Adobe Photoshop, Adobe Dimensions **PAPER:** Mohawk Navajo, Mohawk Tomohawk **COLORS:** 4, process (some forms); 2, match (remainder) **PAGES:** 92 plus insert **SIZE:** 9" x 7¾" (22.8cm x 20cm) **PRINT RUN:** 3,000 **COST:** Paper and printing were donated. **TYPEFACES:** HTF Ziggurat (The Hoefler Type Foundry), Giza (The Font Bureau), Mrs. Eaves (Emigre) **INSPIRATION:** "A New Orleans-style spicy mix." **CONCEPT:** "I wanted to create a spirited, yet useful, conference program," says art director Alexander Isley. "I've been to too many conferences where the programs have been indecipherable. This is a particular problem at design conferences, where the design of the program is often calculated to impress but not inform. Our goal was to create an organized, logical, cheap piece, providing a guide to the AIGA's biannual conference. Our mandate was to make the guide a keepsake. I think our biggest contribution was in the organization of the information, attempting to give an at-a-glance reflection of the spirit of the conference. And it's fun to read." **SPECIAL PRODUCTION TECHNIQUES:** Die-cut divider tabs including recipe cards, cocktail menus and voodoo dolls. The slipcase is also die-cut. **SPECIAL FEATURE:** A foldout mini-conference guide tucks into a die-cut slot on the back cover.

CONTENTS

OFFICIAL JAMBALAYA SEAT HOLDER

Instructions

November 13-16 '97

This Seat Is Saved

EXHIBITIONS
Competitions are documented in exhibitions at the AIGA's Strathmore Gallery. Exhibitions also travel to selected AIGA chapters around the country.

CENTER FOR DESIGN
The AIGA's headquarters, located in the center of the design and technology communities of New York, host a variety of programs and exhibitions in an effort to lead business, the media, and the general public to a better understanding of the value of graphic design. All events are previewed by members, and entry fees are discounted for members.

DESIGN COMPETITIONS
AIGA-sponsored competitions celebrate excellence within the profession and, through their respective annuals and exhibitions, tell a story about the current state of graphic design. There are at least four juried competitions each year, currently including: *Fifty Books/Fifty Covers; Communication Graphics; The Design of Understanding; The Greening of Design;* and *Sound Off: The Top 100 CDs, Music Videos and Print Collateral.* Members benefit from discounted entry fees and advance notice.

INSURANCE
The AIGA offers health, life and disability insurance options to members who might otherwise have difficulty finding local alternatives.

PROFESSIONAL PRACTICE
The AIGA is an excellent resource for information regarding professional practice questions, with assistance available from local chapter networks.

JOIN AIGA

Make something of it
AIGA
Call 212-807-1990

STUDIO: VWA Group, Dallas, TX **ART DIRECTOR/DESIGNER:** Ashley Barron **PHOTOGRAPHY:** Stock **CLIENT/PRODUCT:** Jefferson Properties/luxury apartment homes **SOFTWARE:** QuarkXPress, Adobe Illustrator, Adobe Photoshop **PAPER:** Genesis Birch, Outback Crocodile Corrugate **COLORS:** 4, process plus 2, match **SIZE:** 7 ¼" x 5 ⅛" (18.5cm x 12.8cm) (folded) **PRINT RUN:** 5,000 **COST PER UNIT:** US$5.50 **TYPEFACE:** Berkeley **INSPIRATION:** "This property is set in a beautiful part of California and features Spanish Mission-style architecture," says designer Ashley Barron. "The natural appeal of the surrounding locale served as the primary inspiration for this design." **CONCEPT:** "Because the property was in California, I wanted to stress the beauty of the area but also its casual approach to life. The surprising incorporation of the corrugated paper stock, the notecards included within the package, the four-color printing on uncoated/recycled stock, the raffia tie, etc., all worked together to convey a sense of casual elegance." **SPECIAL FEATURES:** "The brochure is a smaller-scale accordion-fold piece printed on recycled paper. A corrugated sleeve created a sophisticated wrapper to hold the brochure and matching notecards. The wrapper was sealed using raffia and topped off with a dried leaf."

STUDIO: Karacters Design Group, Vancouver, British Columbia, Canada **CREATIVE DIRECTORS:** Gae Wakabayashi, Maria Kennedy **ART DIRECTOR/DESIGNER:** Michelle Melenchuk **PHOTOGRAPHER:** Clinton Hussey **CLIENT:** The Stanley Theatre Society **SOFTWARE:** QuarkXPress **COLORS:** 4 over 2, process plus 2, match **PAGES:** 28, plus cover and jacket **SIZE:** 4 1/4" x 9" (10.8cm x 22.8cm) **PRINT RUN:** 600 **TYPEFACES:** New Baskerville, Helvetica Condensed Black **CONCEPT:** "We wanted to create a sense of immediacy for donations for the renovations of the Stanley Theatre, one of Vancouver's few remaining Art Deco showpieces," say the designers. "It was a challenge to make the piece entertaining and stand out from the multitudes of requests for donations for our target audience. The cover image of a pen, on a brochure the same size as a checkbook, all enclosed in a protective jacket, contributes a subliminal message. We used fictitious and humorous quotes that support the idea of the importance of live theater, and of donating to the cause." **SPECIAL PRODUCTION TECHNIQUES:** Spot varnish on a swirling pattern printed in off-white creates an elegant background for the image of an expensive fountain pen. A die-cut half circle in the sleeve helps recipients remove the brochure. An embossed lip around the gold-and-white title adds further elegance.

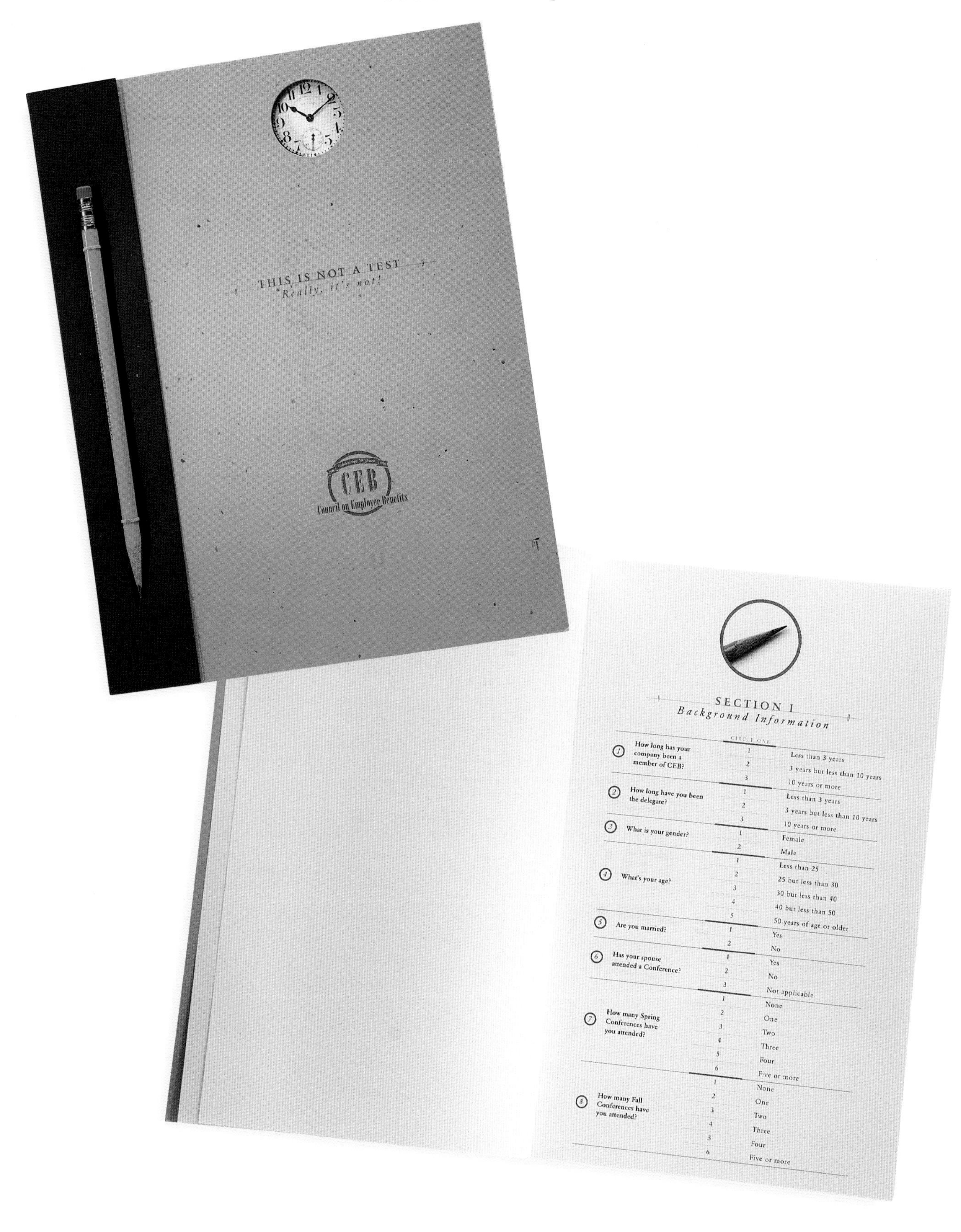

STUDIO: KINETIK Communication Graphics, Inc., Washington, DC **ART DIRECTORS:** Samuel Shelton, Jeffrey Fabian **DESIGNER:** Mimi Masse **CLIENT/SERVICE:** Watson Wyatt Worldwide/consulting **SOFTWARE:** QuarkXPress **PAPER:** Champion Celebration, Circa Select **COLORS:** 1, match (cover); 2, match (interior) **PAGES:** 12 plus cover **SIZE:** 11" x 8½" (28cm x 21.6cm) **PRINT RUN:** 325 **COST PER UNIT:** US$48.60 (includes design, printing and assembly) **TYPEFACE:** New Baskerville **INSPIRATION:** Standardized tests. **CONCEPT:** "To create a unique and memorable presentation for a utilitarian product (a survey) by disguising it as something it's not," says art director Sam Shelton. **SPECIAL PRODUCTION TECHNIQUES:** "A die-cut circle on the cover reveals the clock image on page one. Binding is with rivets, through which a custom-imprinted pencil is attached with a rubber band. A die-cut slit on the inside back cover holds the return envelope." **SPECIAL FOLDS:** "The back cover folds back on itself to allow for a die-cut slit, which holds a return envelope. The back cover also wraps around the front to create a double-thick spine, through which the rivets are attached."

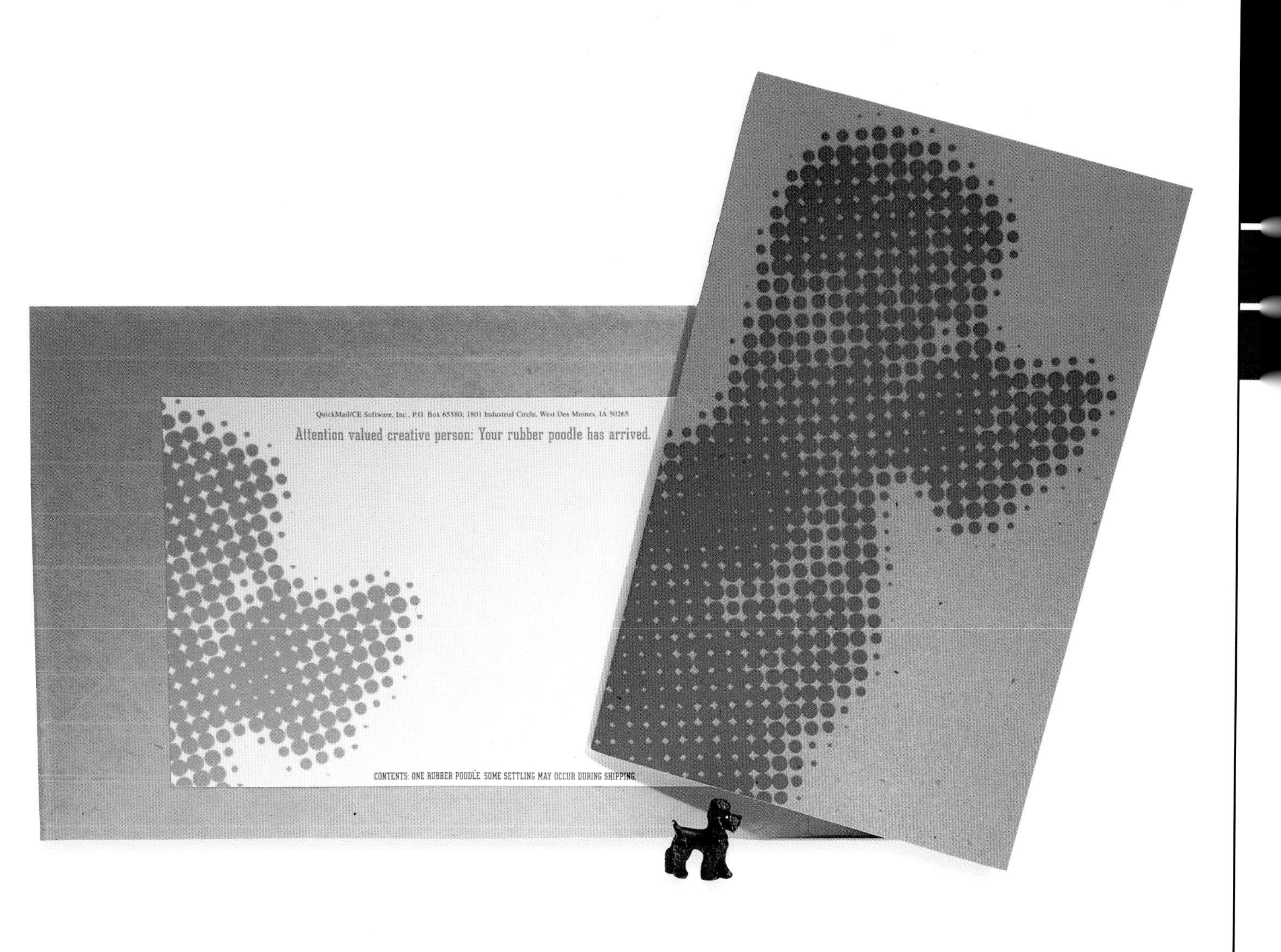

QuickMail/CE Software, Inc., P.O. Box 65580, 1801 Industrial Circle, West Des Moines, IA 50265
Attention valued creative person: Your rubber poodle has arrived.
CONTENTS: ONE RUBBER POODLE. SOME SETTLING MAY OCCUR DURING SHIPPING.

STUDIO: Planet Design Company, Madison, WI **ART DIRECTOR:** Kevin Wade **DESIGNER:** Martha Graettinger **CLIENT/SERVICE:** CE Software/E-mail software **SOFTWARE:** QuarkXPress, Adobe Illustrator **PAPER:** Fox River Confetti **COLORS:** 4, match **SIZE:** 8" x 5" (20.3cm x 12.8cm) **CONCEPT:** "Through clever copywriting and the use of bold type and color," says designer Martha Graettinger, grabbing "the attention of resellers of E-mail software and setting them up for a special sales promotion." **SPECIAL FEATURES:** The graphic design features a dot-screen image of a rubber poodle, which was included in the promo as a tongue-in-cheek incentive.

ART DIRECTOR/DESIGNER: Anne-Lise Dermenghem, Neuilly-Sur-Seine, France **CLIENT/SERVICE:** Actia/association for the French food industry **SOFTWARE:** Adobe Photoshop, Adobe Illustrator, QuarkXPress **PAPER:** Conoisseur **COLORS:** 4, process plus 1, match (brochure); 2, match (card) **PAGES:** 8 (brochure) **SIZE:** 6 ½" x 9 ⅜" (16.5cm x 24cm) (brochure); 5 ½" x 5 ½" (14cm x 14cm) (card) **PRINT RUN:** 3,000 (brochure), 300 (card) **COST PER UNIT:** Fr 22 (brochure), Fr 24 (card) **TYPEFACES:** Friz Quadrata (Actia logo); Meta (brochure); Goudy (card) **CONCEPT:** "Explaining Actia's dynamism, and evoking the different research centers that cover all the sectors of the food industry." **SPECIAL PRODUCTION TECHNIQUE:** The brochure pages feature a central circular die-cut that reveals Actia's logo on the inside cover. A plastic window in the card's face covers colored confetti and, again, the logo. Both pieces were hand-assembled at a workshop employing the mentally handicapped. "I made all the confetti myself from colored paper, during long evenings!" says designer Anne-Lise Dermenghem.

STUDIO: Levine & Associates, Washington, DC **ART DIRECTORS:** John Vance, Laura Latham **DESIGNER:** Laura Latham **ILLUSTRATOR:** Interface Multimedia (fold-out architectural rendering) **CLIENT/SERVICE:** Apco Worldwide/public affairs **SOFTWARE:** QuarkXPress, Adobe Illustrator, Adobe Photoshop **PAPER:** Eco Board (black box), Cadillac Silk Embossed Silver (cover), UV Ultra Opalescent Gray (endpaper), Potlatch McCoy Gloss (text) **COLORS:** 6 over 6; 4, process plus match blue and match metallic silver **PAGES:** 18, plus endpapers and cover **SIZE:** 12¾" x 9⅞" x 1¼" (25.1cm x 32.2cm x 3.2cm)(box); 10" x 7¾" (25.5cm x 19.7cm)(brochure) **PRINT RUN:** 3,500 **COST PER UNIT:** US$22 **TYPEFACES:** Bank Gothic, Weiss **INSPIRATION:** "Technological and human achievement in aviation and space exploration," says art director John Vance, who wanted to capture "a monumental vision for celebrating that achievement." **CONCEPT:** "Using materials, finishing and formats to reflect those of air and space technology. Using fold-outs to reflect the expansiveness of the museum collection and facility. Using inspiring quotes from prominent individuals to reflect the historic importance of the subject." **SPECIAL PRODUCTION TECHNIQUES:** "The box is custom-fabricated to hold a brochure, video and funding proposal. The box is foil-stamped, and a pattern of air and spacecraft profiles is debossed on it. The brochure is bound with grommets, and a quotation is embossed on the cover." **SPECIAL FOLDS OR FEATURES:** Two brochure pages each fold out twice.

STUDIO: Dupla Design, Rio de Janeiro, Brazil **DESIGNERS:** Ney Valle, Claudia Gamboa **PHOTOGRAPHERS:** Cesar Barreto, Kadu Niemeyer, Magno Mesquita, Marcelo Ribeiro **CLIENT:** Museum of Contemporary Art of Niterói **SOFTWARE:** Macromedia PageMaker, Adobe Photoshop **PAPER:** Gainsborough Silver (cover), Couche matte (interior) **COLORS:** 2, match (cover); 4, process (interior) **PAGES:** 56 **SIZE:** 11¾" x 8⅜" (29.9cm x 21.2cm)(pamphlet) **PRINT RUN:** 1,500 **COST PER UNIT:** R$25,70 **TYPEFACE:** Frutiger **INSPIRATION:** "Oscar Niemeyer's architecture," says designer Ney Valle, "its simplicity and objectivity; his materials, curves and spaces." **CONCEPT:** "This piece presents a contemporary museum and must represent its architecture and collections." **SPECIAL FEATURES:** At the museum's opening, a plastic and cardboard sack held the catalog and other print pieces. The bag was printed with the museum's logo, and the handle was die-cut a similar shape. The letters "MAC" (Museu de Arte Contemporânea) are embossed on the cover.

O Museu de Arte Contemporânea de Niterói é um projeto do arquiteto Oscar Niemeyer, apresentado pela primeira vez à imprensa em 15 de julho de 1991, por seu autor e pelo então prefeito Jorge Roberto Silveira. Foi construído em 6 anos, durante duas administrações municipais: a de Jorge Roberto e a de João Sampaio.

A idéia de construir um museu de arte contemporânea foi provocada pela promessa de cessão, por comodato de João Sattamini, da sua coleção de arte, composta de cerca de 1000 peças entre pinturas, desenhos, esculturas, objetos, instalações, dos mais representativos artistas brasileiros das últimas quatro décadas.

O projeto cultural foi coordenado pela Secretaria Municipal da Cultura e pela Fundação Niteroiense de Arte-Funiarte. A obra ficou sob a direção, orientação e controle da Emusa, empresa da Prefeitura de Niterói.

MUSEU DE ARTE CONTEMPORÂNEA DE NITERÓI

Sua forma inusitada e bela -uma estrutura de concreto sobre uma praça de 2.500 m2, situada no mirante da Boa Viagem, entre as praias Vermelha e das Flechas, próximo dos bairros históricos de Gragoatá e São Domingos- tem sido divulgada no Brasil, EUA e Europa. Para a exposição itinerante dos Prêmios Pritzker, EUA, o "Nobel de Arquitetura", o arquiteto Oscar Niemeyer, premiado em 1988 escolheu a maquete do MAC Niterói para representar sua obra. A revista britânica *World Architecture* e *Ufficiostile* de Milão já lhe dedicaram páginas e capa , nos últimos anos.

A leveza aparente da arquitetura do MAC Niterói resulta da concentração complexa de todo o arcabouço de concreto armado em um apoio central, que serve também de circulação vertical de serviço, entre o subsolo e os dois andares de exposição (cerca de 2.000m2), além da varanda periférica de onde se descortinam os recôncavos de Niterói, o Pão de Açúcar, a Pedra da Gávea e o penhasco do Corcovado. A administração, está localizadas no primeiro andar. O projeto e a ambientação dos interiores foi concebido, e presenteado à cidade, pela designer Anna Maria Niemeyer.

No subsolo, além da reserva técnica devidamente protegida do calor e da umidade, situa-se, voltado para a Guanabara, um restaurante, com acesso público independente, cujo *hall* e bar servem também ao auditório destina à conferências, debates e eventos áudio visuais.

A circulação do público é feita pela grande rampa com 98 metros de extensão, cujas curvas, que parecem voar, servem para apreciar a grande forma branca, repentinamente refletida no espelho d'água de onde brota o conjunto, criando-se mais uma relação onírica entre o mar, o panorama e a construção cultural.

Designed by world-famous architect Oscar Niemeyer, the Niterói Contemporary Art Museum was presented to the Press for the first time on 15 July 1991, by its designer and the Mayor of Niterói at that time, Jorge Roberto Silveira. It was built over the course of six years, during two municipal administrations, the first headed by Jorge Roberto Silveira and the second under Mayor João Sampaio.

The idea of building a Contemporary Art Museum was prompted by the promise of João Sattamini to endow it on permanent loan with his Contemporary Art Collection, consisting of some 1,000 items, including paintings, drawings, sculptures, objects, and installations representing a wide variety of Brazilian artists over the past four decades.

This cultural project was coordinated by the Municipal Culture Bureau and the Niterói Art Foundation - FUNIARTE - *Fundação Niteroiense de Arte*. The works were managed, supervised and controlled by Emusa, a company run by the Niterói Prefecture.

Its unusual shape is eye-catching - a concrete structure set in a plaza covering 2,500 square meters on the Boa Viagem look-out point between the Vermelha and Flechas beaches and close to the historical districts of Gragoatá and São Domingos - and has received much attention in Brazil, the U.S.A. and Europe.

Architect Oscar Niemeyer selected the maquette of the Niterói Contemporary Art Museum for the Pritzker Awards Traveling Exhibition in the U.S.A., often known as the Nobel Prize of Architecture. The British magazine *World Architecture* and Milan's *Ufficiostile* have already dedicated many pages and covers to this project, over the past few years.

The apparent lightness of the architecture of the Niterói Contemporary Art Museum is the outcome of a complex concentration of the entire reinforced concrete framework on a central core, which also serves as the vertical service area between the basement and the two exhibition floors (covering some 2,000 square meters). Surrounded by a verandah, it offers breath-taking views of the Niterói coastline, the Sugar Loaf, the cliffs of Corcovado topped by Christ the Redeemer, and other landmarks such as the flat-topped Pedra da Gávea. Its offices are located on the first floor, and its interior decor was conceptualized and presented to the City by designer Ana Maria Niemeyer.

In addition to the storerooms - properly protected from heat and humidity - the basement also houses a restaurant, with independent public access and a view over the Guanabara Bay. The lobby and bar also serve as an auditorium for conferences, discussions and audio-visual events.

Public access is along a massive ramp 98 meters long, whose curves seem to soar through the air. This is the perfect place to admire the huge white shape which suddenly appears, reflected in the pool of water at the foot of this complex, creating yet another dreamlike relationship between the sea, the landscape and this cultural center.

8

EXPOSIÇÃO INAUGURAL
Arte Contemporânea Brasileira na Coleção João Sattamini

Maria Auxiliadora Silveira
Maurício Elias Caldas
Marcia Maria Muller
Coordenação

Reynaldo Roels Jr.
Curadoria

Fátima Henriques
Helenice Dornelles
Katia Ribeiro da Costa e Silva
Telma Lasmar
Montagem

Peter Gasper
Iluminação

Heloisa Assad
Maude Monnerat
Assistentes da coordenação

Luana Teixeira
Estagiária

Adão de Oliveira
Jorge Davi da Costa
José Marcos Serrano
Moacir
Roberto de Oliveira
Apoio operacional

Cristina Pape
Studiorestauro, RJ
Conservação das obras de arte

Aparecida Rollemberg
Lúcia Rito
Beatriz Horta
Divulgação

CATÁLOGO

Cesar Barreto (obras de arte)
Claudio Cardoso
Kadu Niemeyer
Magno Mesquita
Marcelo Ribeiro
Fotografias

Caroly Brissett
Patricia Tate
Versão inglês

Dupla Ney Valle/ Claudia Gamboa
Projeto Gráfico

...SEU DE ARTE CONTEMPORÂNEA DE NITERÓI
...rio de funcionamento
...rça a sábado, das 13:00 h às 21:00 h
...ngos, das 13:00 h às 19:00 h
...da Boa Viagem, s/nº - Niterói - RJ - Brasil
...1) 620-2400/620-2481
...etrônico
...w.actech.com.br/macnit

" ...hoje aflorando do espelho d'água que é um eco do mar – como um firme caule que se abre em flor – chama cálice?"

Foi num dia ameno, em 1991, devia ser maio. Eu acompanhava o arquiteto Oscar Niemeyer e o prefeito Jorge Roberto Silveira, buscando na orla marítima um terreno adequado ao Museu de Arte Contemporânea de Niterói. Mas no meio do caminho, no mirante da Boa Viagem, já era evidente que o Destino acertara. Seria ali o museu que ainda não tinha forma, mas nascia coma a vocação de ser, invicta até hoje.

Apenas uma semana antes, eu recebera na Secretaria da Cultura, uma visita inusitada. Anna Maria Niemeyer, amiga de toda a vida, trazia-me João Sattamini, colecionador famoso e Victor Arruda, pintor de uma força danada, mas vindo aqui como curador da mítica Coleção Sattamini

It was a mild day in 1991, perhaps in May. I was accompanying architect Oscar Niemeyer and Mayor Jorge Roberto Silveira as we hunted for an appropriate site for the Niterói Contemporary Art Museum along the coastline. But along the way, at the Boa Viagem look-out point, it became clear that destiny had already made up its mind. This was to be the site of the Museum which as yet had no shape, but which was born with the vocation to "be", still today unconquered. Just one week earlier, I had received an unexpected visitor at the Board of Culture. My life-long friend Anna Maria Niemeyer brought famous art collector João Sattamini to meet me, together with Victor Arruda, a powerful painter, but present that day as the Curator of the mythical Sattamini Collection, a treasure trove of unlimited profusion and dizzying scope that had never been seen in public or even accurately measured. They wanted to house this fabulous potential in Niterói. Deeply involved, they were looking for an old, but refurbished building, as funding was limited to the reigning dream of the cultural marketing world. I admit that I was skeptical at first, but nevertheless keenly aware that I worked there at the invitation of an outstanding Mayor for whom no beauty or grandeur was too much for Niterói. We enjoyed looking through the old Government buildings available, none of which fitted the sophisticated dreams of the visitors, due either to their size or disparity of historical use. The conventionally ugly Public Depository pleased the aesthetics of Victor, but could not be used due to its ruinous condition and poor location, at the foot of the bridge spanning the Bay from the viewpoint of Niterói. What about the old Tram Station? The Masonry Yard? It was obviously urgent to bring this matter before the Mayor. One day later, the future had already been outlined. Jorge Roberto Silveira, who is not one for half-measures, commissioned me to invite Oscar Niemeyer and see if he would like to build a Contemporary Art Museum in Niterói. I called on Anna Maria Niemeyer, at her art gallery, to outline the scope of this project. The entire

- acervo de profusão ilimitada e vertiginoso alcance, mas até então jamais visto ou medido ao certo. E eles queriam abrigar esse potencial fabuloso em Niterói. Apaixonados, queriam um velho prédio recuperado, mas quanto a recursos só se podia contar com a fantasia reinante do mundo do marketing cultural. Confesso que fui cético no primeiro momento, mas sabendo muito bem que trabalhava aqui convocado por um prefeito excepcional, para quem nenhuma beleza ou grandeza seria demais em Niterói. Percorremos com muito prazer os velhos prédios públicos que correspondiam, pelo vulto ou disparidade de uso histórico, ao sonho sofisticado dos visitantes. O Depósito Público, convencionalmente feio, convinha à estética de Victor, mas não servia, de tão arruinado e mal

Italo Campofiorito

14

15

STUDIO: Tcherevkoff Studio Ltd., New York, NY **ART DIRECTOR:** Michel Tcherevkoff **DESIGNER:** Howard Huang **PHOTOGRAPHER:** Michel Tcherevkoff **CLIENT:** Self; Bed, Bath & Beyond (featured) **SOFTWARE:** Barco Creator, Adobe Photoshop, Adobe Illustrator **PAPER:** Epson Photo Quality Inject Card, vellum **COLORS:** 6, process **PAGES:** 9 **SIZE:** 4 ⅛" x 6" (10.5cm x 15.2cm) **PRINT RUN:** 500 **COST PER UNIT:** US$7–8 **TYPEFACE:** Havelica **INSPIRATION:** "To have a mini portfolio to show my mother in France what I was doing!!!" says art director Michel Tcherevkoff. **CONCEPT:** "Highlighting one of my current advertising campaigns." Bright images showcase the designs, while corrugated covers and vellum flyleaves add elegance. **SPECIAL PRODUCTION TECHNIQUES:** "Self-production with Epson Stylus Photo Ex and HP LaserWriter 5MP." **SPECIAL FEATURES:** A handmade "die-cut" in the glossy green protective card gives a glimpse of the bright yellow corrugated paper. The piece was mailed in a transparent plastic envelope.

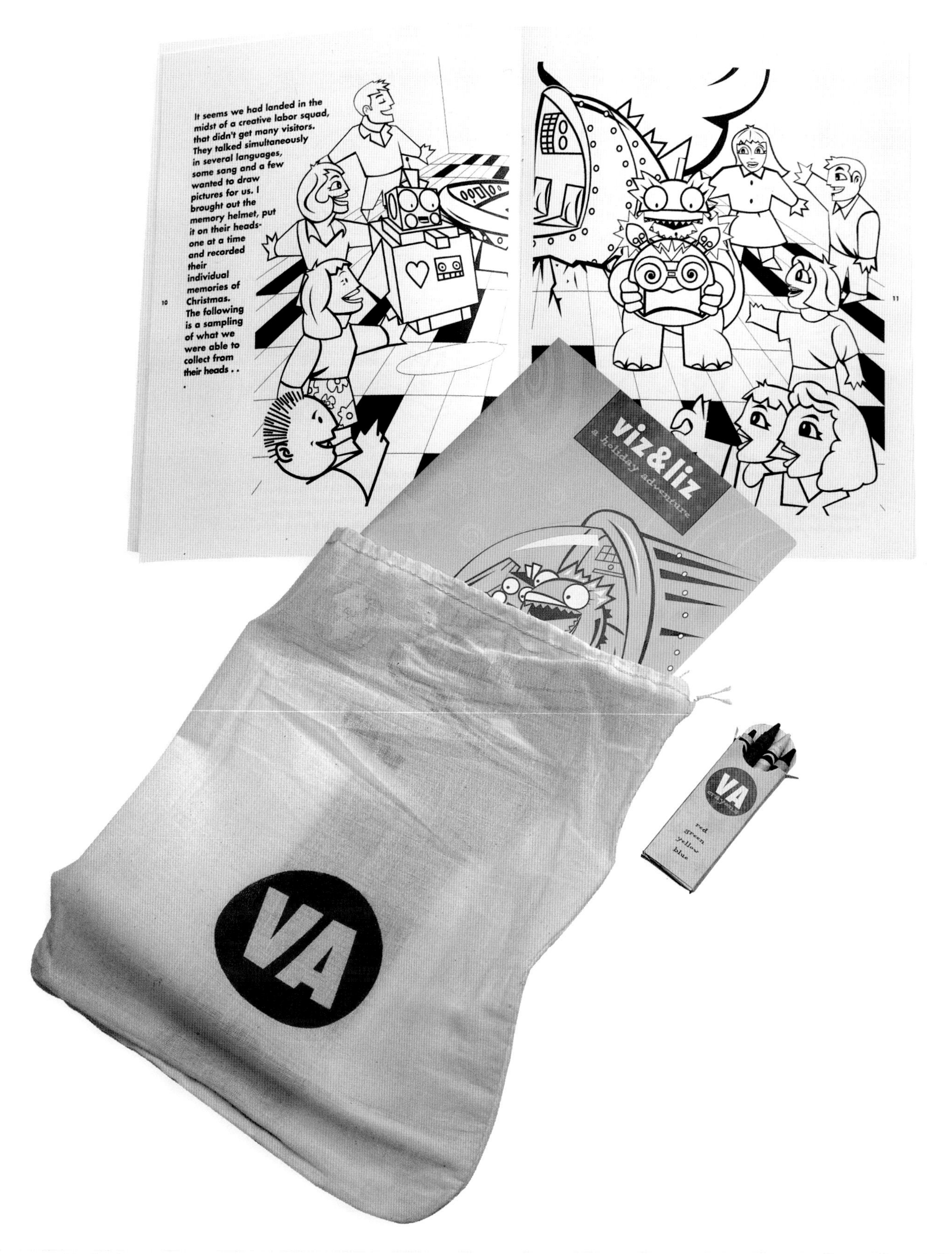

It seems we had landed in the midst of a creative labor squad, that didn't get many visitors. They talked simultaneously in several languages, some sang and a few wanted to draw pictures for us. I brought out the memory helmet, put it on their heads- one at a time and recorded their individual memories of Christmas. The following is a sampling of what we were able to collect from their heads . .
10
11
viz&liz
a holiday adventure
VA
VA
red
green
yellow
blue

STUDIO: Visual Asylum, San Diego, CA **ART DIRECTORS:** MaeLin Levine, Amy Jo Levine **DESIGNERS:** Charles Glaubitz, Joel Sotelo, Paul Drohan **ILLUSTRATOR:** Charles Glaubitz **COPYWRITER:** Troy Viss **CLIENT:** Self **SOFTWARE:** QuarkXPress, Adobe Illustrator **PAPER:** French Butcher Paper **COLORS:** 4, process (cover); black (interior) **PAGES:** 40 **SIZE:** 11" x 8½" (28cm x 21.6cm) **PRINT RUN:** 200 **TYPEFACE:** Futura **INSPIRATION:** "Childhood memories of the holiday season," says art director MaeLin Levine. **CONCEPT:** "To create fictitious characters who land on Earth at Visual Asylum and want to learn about the spirit of the holiday season. The characters visit each team member's memory for an individual interpretation of the season." **SPECIAL PRODUCTION TECHNIQUES:** The total holiday package included the coloring book, crayons with VA wrappers, and a miniature train, all packaged in a cloth bag screenprinted with the studio's logo and sealed with a huge red tag. **SPECIAL COST-CUTTING TECHNIQUES:** "The contents of the coloring book were printed in black on newsprint. The book cover and crayon box were printed together on the same press sheet, then the crayon labels were laser printed and hand-applied."

STUDIO: Design Narrative Ltd., London, U.K. **ART DIRECTOR:** Andy Ewan **DESIGNERS:** Design Narrative Ltd. **CLIENT:** Self **PAPER:** Cyclus **COLORS:** Black plus match metallic silver **PAGES:** 12 **SIZE:** 3 ½" x 2 ⅜" (9cm x 6cm) **PRINT RUN:** 1,000 **COST PER UNIT:** UK£1 **INSPIRATION:** "$e = mc^2$" **CONCEPT:** "The language of creativity," says art director Andy Ewan. Pocket-sized, black-and-white booklets in tiny, brightly colored envelopes encourage creativity.

STUDIO: Dupla Design, Rio de Janeiro, Brazil **DESIGNERS:** Ney Valle, Claudia Gamboa, Fernanda Paes **PHOTOGRAPHERS:** Mario Grisolli, Fausto Fleury, Odervan Santiago **CLIENT:** Museum of Contemporary Art of Niterói **SOFTWARE:** Macromedia PageMaker, Adobe Photoshop **PAPER:** Triplex, Couche matte **COLORS:** 2, match (text); 4, process (postcards) **PAGES:** 16 plus cover and 12 postcards **SIZE:** 12 3/8" x 7" (31.5cm x 17.9cm) **PRINT RUN:** 1,500 **COST PER UNIT:** R$6,70 **TYPEFACES:** Orator, Gold **INSPIRATION:** "Mirrors, and the kind of tickets for exhibitions like the Bienal," says designer Ney Valle. **CONCEPT:** The exhibit featured works from the young museum's collections that have been shown at São Paulo Bienals, holding a "mirror" both to those exhibitions and the evolution of contemporary art. According to Valle, the concept was "to create a contemporary, versatile piece within a limited budget." Twelve postcards add color to the piece, also serving as keepsakes. **SPECIAL FEATURES:** The cover, printed in metallic silver, is die-cut and perforated into squares. The inside pages are printed to mimic perforations. The Portuguese text is printed in straight columns and capital letters. English text, in narrow tilted columns, is printed in a spring green.

STUDIO: Dupla Design, Rio de Janeiro, Brazil **DESIGNERS:** Ney Valle, Claudia Gamboa, Fernanda Paes **PHOTOGRAPHERS:** Wilton Montenegro, Sebastio Barbosa, Pedro Oswaldo Cruz **CLIENT:** Museum of Contemporary Art of Niterói **SOFTWARE:** Macromedia PageMaker, Adobe Photoshop **PAPER:** Cardboard (package/cover), Couche matte **COLORS:** Black (screen-printed package/cover); 4, process (booklets) **PAGES:** 16 (part 1), 16 (part 2) plus folder/introduction **SIZE:** 8 5/8" x 8 11/16" (22cm x 22.1 cm)(package/cover); 8 1/8" x 8 1/4" (20.5cm x 21cm)(booklets) **PRINT RUN:** 1,500 **COST PER UNIT:** R$9,00 **TYPEFACES:** Confidential, Frutiger **INSPIRATION:** "The work, the projects for the exhibition/installation, and the personality of each artist," according to designer Ney Valle. **CONCEPT:** "Working with the box, its textures, and the discoveries within it, to convey the sense of works in progress, handmade by artists. Also, preserving the personality and style of work of each artist, but creating a single result."

artur barrio

OCUPAÇÕES

artur barrio
antonio manuel

DESCOBRIMENTOS

Sometimes it's easy to forget that brochures don't have to be printed paper. Or at least not exclusively. Or at least not just plain paper. Your printer knows all kinds of tricks—die-cuts, embossing or debossing, unusual bindings and folds. And what your printer doesn't know about interesting fasteners, your local hardware store clerk just might be able to tell you. Of course, most of these techniques cost a little more. But not all of them. And even when they cost an arm and a leg, they'll be worth it for the right client.

[special production techniques]

[special production techniques] 4

in this chapter, you'll see how:

- Brainstorm designers screen-printed sheets of rubber for a brochure cover that has the same great smell as a playground ball.
- Designers at Visual Asylum used a humble wing nut as a design symbol, as well as a nifty way to hold a bunch of papers together.
- "Mr." Tharp at Tharp Did It! included a client's product on its brochure cover, letting recipients see the product immediately.

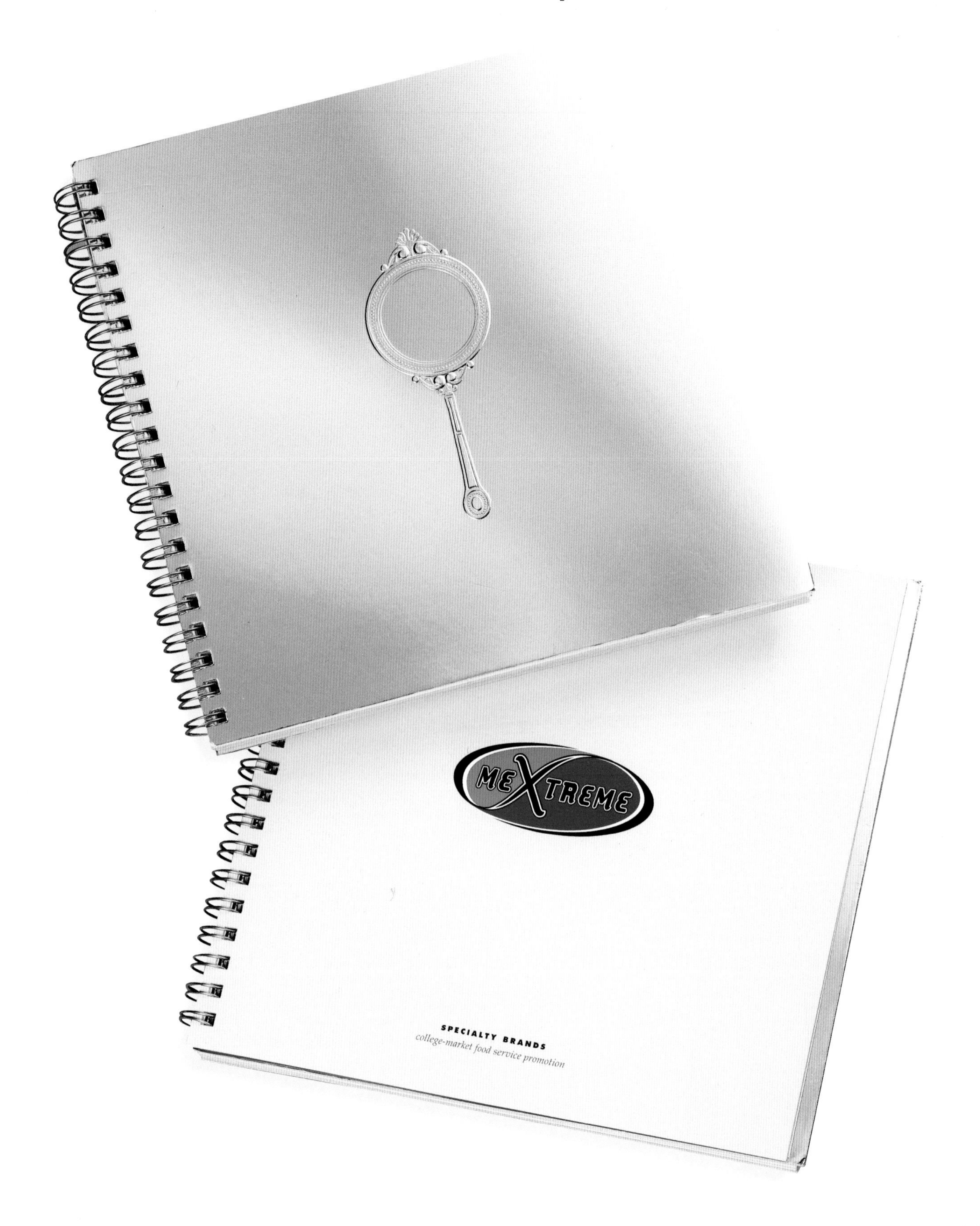

STUDIO: Mires Design Inc., San Diego, CA **ART DIRECTOR:** John Ball **DESIGNER:** Gale Spitzley **ILLUSTRATORS:** Miguel Perez, Jeff Samaripa **CLIENT:** Self **SOFTWARE:** QuarkXPress, Adobe Illustrator **PAPER:** Zanders Mirricard Silver (cover); Zanders Chromolux Vario Cover, Red (interior) **COLORS:** 4, process **PAGES:** 30 plus cover **SIZE:** 7" x 7 1/8" (17.8cm x 18.1cm) **PRINT RUN:** 1,000 **INSPIRATION:** "Our mission, which is to make every identity a unique reflection of an organization or product's best qualities," say the designers. **CONCEPT:** "The book is used to present our work to potential clients, both delivered in person and by direct mail. We used a mirror-like cover stock to reflect our philosophy on corporate and brand identity." **SPECIAL FEATURES:** Both front and back covers are embossed. The interior paper stock makes a striking impression—the glossy white surface showcases the printed graphics and contrasts strongly with the matte red surface.

STUDIO: Brainstorm, Inc., Dallas, TX **ART DIRECTORS/DESIGNERS:** Chuck Johnson, Tom Kirsch, Adam Hallmark, Ryan Martin **ILLUSTRATORS:** Chuck Johnson, Tom Kirsch, Adam Hallmark, Ryan Martin **PHOTOGRAPHER:** Doug Davis **CLIENT:** Self **SOFTWARE:** QuarkXPress, Adobe Illustrator, Adobe Photoshop **PAPER:** French Dur-o-Tone Butcher, Potlatch McCoy Cover **COLORS:** 4, process plus satin varnish **PAGES:** 36 plus cover **SIZE:** 10" x 6½" (25.4cm x 16.5cm) **PRINT RUN:** 500 **TYPEFACES:** Clarendon, AG Old Face, Tarzana, DIN Engschrift, News Gothic **INSPIRATION:** "To show off good design and concept," says designer Chuck Johnson. **CONCEPT:** "Brainstorm's corporate tagline is 'We Think. You'll See.' There are two sections. The 'We Think' section is about corporate philosophy and the creative process. The 'You'll See' section is the portfolio. The Brainstorm graphic spiral is used throughout in different treatments as subtle yet fun branding." **SPECIAL PRODUCTION TECHNIQUES:** Wire-o binding, done in-house, makes it easy to update. **SPECIAL FEATURE:** Screen-printed rubber cover.

STUDIO: Tharp Did It!, Los Gatos, CA **ART DIRECTOR:** Mr. Tharp **DESIGNERS:** Gina Kim-Mageras, Nicole Coleman **ILLUSTRATOR:** Carl Yoshihara **COPYWRITER:** Writerguy (Ken Eklund) **CLIENT/PRODUCT:** Cellotape, Inc./labels, name-plates, overlay panels **SOFTWARE:** Adobe Illustrator, Adobe Photoshop **PAPER:** Simpson EverGreen Gloss cover **COLORS:** 4, match plus black **PAGES:** 12 **SIZE:** 6 ¾" x 4" (17.2cm x 10.1cm) **PRINT RUN:** 10,000 **TYPEFACE:** Officina **INSPIRATION:** "Dictated by the message," says Mr. Tharp. "The writer and art director worked very closely to ensure that nothing got in the way of the story that needed to be told. Hence, big type and clear visuals." **CONCEPT:** "To create a handheld reference guide. The type is big and bold and gives the mini-brochure a larger presence. The concept for the cover was to apply an actual Cellotape product to the cover, to immediately show the viewer what the company manufactures." **SPECIAL PRODUCTION TECHNIQUES:** "The cover of the brochure is an actual plastic face panel for a cell phone. It features a clear window, through which a part of the first page can be read." **SPECIAL FOLDS:** "The center spread is a gatefold that features diagrams of high-tech equipment supported by the company's nameplate and labeling solutions." **SPECIAL COST-CUTTING TECHNIQUES:** "The brochure was printed by a local printer, but the cover panel was produced and applied by the client. We wanted to show off the client's own techniques for embossing, die-cutting and creating special finishes."

BAND: JACK O' FIRE

TITLE: PUNKIN'

LABEL: ESTRUS RECORDS, 1994

Imagine blues/soul shoved through fifteen years of punk rock recorded with broken equipment on a dictaphone machine and then you might understand what these guys sound like. They collected Halloween and voodoo parapher-nalia, so a diecut jack-o'-lantern (a.k.a. Jack O' Fire) with glow-in-the-dark vinyl peeking through seemed a natural choice for the design.

STUDIO: Chantry/Sheehan, Seattle, WA **ART DIRECTORS/DESIGNERS:** Jamie Sheehan, Art Chantry **PHOTOGRAPHER:** Michels Studio **CLIENT:** Appleton Papers **SOFTWARE:** QuarkXPress, Adobe Photoshop, Macromedia FreeHand **PAPER:** Appleton Papers Utopia One dull cover and text gloss **COLORS:** 4, process plus 2 varnishes **PAGES:** 26 **SIZE:** 6¾" x 6¾" (17.2cm x 17.2cm) **PRINT RUN:** 15,000 **TYPEFACES:** Adobe Garamond (body), Copperplate 29 A-B (credits) **INSPIRATION:** "45 rpm records and sleeves," says designer Art Chantry. **CONCEPT:** A promo tie-in to the AIGA CD-100 show, it showcases Art Chantry's cover art (mostly for 45 rpm records) for bands (mostly punk). **SPECIAL PRODUCTION TECHNIQUES:** "A very anal atten-tion to detail," says Chantry. "Note the wear rings on the design, giving the piece a thrift store quality—on purpose!" **SPECIAL FEATURES:** A die-cut hole reveals a plastic adapter print-ed on the first page. A "creative advisory" sticker on the black sleeve adds another note of humor. **SPECIAL COST-CUTTING TECHNIQUE:** Although the 'record' is embossed, the 'grooves' are replicated less expensively with varnish.

operation
BWM
BRENTWOOD MALL
no. 1998
military documents inside
IT'S WAR
on our competitors.
ANNUAL GENERAL MEETING
Handout Information
04.21.98
1ST on the agenda
1. Welcome and Call to Order
2. Opening Remarks and President's Message
3. Centre Manager's Comments
4. Approval of Minutes from 1997 AGM
5. Auditor's Report and Financial Statements
6. Appointment of Auditor
7. Election of 1998/99 Board of Directors
8. Marketing Director's Report
9. Election Results
10. 1997 Merchant Achievement Awards
11. Prize Draw
12. Guest Speaker: Dan Charrette, Statistics Canada
13. New Business
14. Adjournment
Divine Dividends a Heavenly STIR
Brentwood Mall launched our Divine Dividends Customer Rewards Program in 1997 with the intent to encourage Brentwood customers to shop more frequently, increase individual expenditures per visit and encourage these goals throughout the year. The incentive was a collectible series of custom-designed Angels created exclusively for Brentwood Mall. Advertised within the shopping centre only, the program boasted over 600 members and represented over $98,000.00 in sales revenue.
Winner of MERIT Maple Leaf Award: Overall Marketing Campaign
This award recognizes a single campaign that combines elements from at least two areas of shopping centre marketing. The category looks for synergy of well-integrated marketing programs that use multiple and varied efforts to benefit their shopping centres. Our 'Make the Season Bright' Christmas campaign integrated sales promotion, consumer advertising, customer relations and community program initiatives to give customers unique reasons to shop at Brentwood Mall.
1997 HIGHLIGHTS
PAGE 3
special EVENTS for 1998
ITEMS TO REMEMBER SO YOU CAN PLAN AHEAD
Youth Week: May
Antique Show: May
Safety Week: June
Sidewalk Sale: July
Back To School Promotion: August/September
Antique Show: September
Halloween Festivities: October
Christmas Promotions: November/December
Sidewalk Sale: January 1999

STUDIO: Big Eye Creative, Vancouver, British Columbia, Canada **ART DIRECTOR/DESIGNER:** Nancy Yeasting **ILLUSTRATOR:** Nancy Yeasting **CLIENT:** Brentwood Mall **SOFTWARE:** Adobe Illustrator, Adobe Photoshop **PAPER:** Blueprint stock **COLORS:** Blueprint blue **PAGES:** 8, one-sided **SIZE:** 12" x 9" (30.5cm x 22.9cm) **PRINT RUN:** 175 **COST PER UNIT:** Can$0.69/US$0.48 **TYPEFACES:** Bureau Gothic (Jonathan Hoefler, David Berlow), Egiziano Black (Vincent Figgins), OCR-A, Meta (Erik Spiekermann), Stamp Gothic (Just van Rossum), Doric Bold (Walter Tracy) **CONCEPT:** "For Brentwood Mall's Annual General Meeting the theme was 'War Against the Competition,' says designer Nancy Yeasting. "I didn't want to focus on the negative aspects of war (I had just seen *Saving Private Ryan*), so I geared it toward the motivating goal of strategy: how one would go about planning a course of action. The concept of blueprint maps came to mind immediately, as well as the thought of using some kind of metal material for binding." **SPECIAL TYPE TECHNIQUES:** "Artwork was supplied as laser-prints, to maintain roughness. Some of the art and graphics were appropriately roughed up on the photocopier. Certain typefaces were chosen because they were graphically rough-edged. Others were chosen because they would retain legibility in the rough printing process." **SPECIAL PRODUCTION TECHNIQUES:** "Our client loved the idea, but she was well acquainted with the undesirable odor of blueprint chemicals left on freshly printed sheets. She suggested that we air out the pages before binding them. The brochure was hand-bound with a two-hole office punch and metal clips from an office stationery store (both used for our job dockets). Once assembled, it was rolled into a cardboard tube that was covered with green camouflage-patterned fabric. They were handed out at the AGM by mall staff who were appropriately dressed in full army camouflage outfits. It was a hit, and a unique project that I'm very proud of."

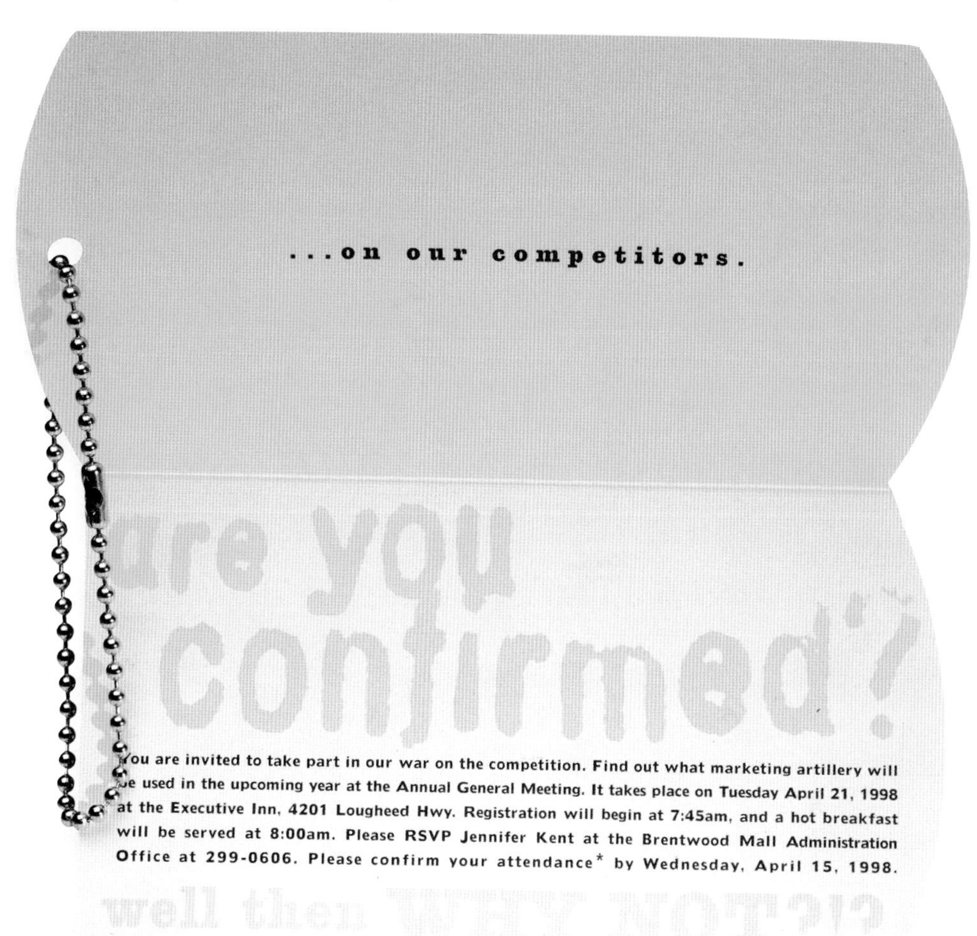

...on our competitors.
are you confirmed?
You are invited to take part in our war on the competition. Find out what marketing artillery will be used in the upcoming year at the Annual General Meeting. It takes place on Tuesday April 21, 1998 at the Executive Inn, 4201 Lougheed Hwy. Registration will begin at 7:45am, and a hot breakfast will be served at 8:00am. Please RSVP Jennifer Kent at the Brentwood Mall Administration Office at 299-0606. Please confirm your attendance* by Wednesday, April 15, 1998.
well then WHY NOT?!?
*If you have confirmed your presence, please be advised that you will be invoiced for the meeting in the event that you do not attend.
We are looking for Nominees for the Brentwood Mall Merchants' Association
Board of Directors. If you or someone else (must be a Brentwood Mall Store
REPORT TO
AGM
HEADQUARTERS AT
TARDINESS IS NOT TOLERATED
AN URGENT MESSAGE
BRENTWOOD MALL
FROM CPL JOLANDA SMITS
0745H
IT'S WAR
WIN
BINOCULARS

STUDIO: Big Eye Creative, Vancouver, British Columbia, Canada **ART DIRECTOR/DESIGNER:** Nancy Yeasting **ILLUSTRATOR:** Nancy Yeasting **CLIENT:** Brentwood Mall **SOFTWARE:** Adobe Illustrator, Adobe Photoshop **PAPER:** Currency Metallic Silver, textured finish (one side coated textured silver finish, the other side smooth white uncoated finish) **COLORS:** Process black **PAGES:** 1 sheet, folded into 3 panels **SIZE:** 3⅜" x 6¼" (8.5cm x 15.9cm) (folded); 10" x 6¼" (25.4cm x 15.9cm) (unfolded) **PRINT RUN:** 175 **COST PER UNIT:** Can$3.45; US$2.41 **TYPEFACES:** Bureau Gothic (Jonathan Hoefler, David Berlow), Doric Bold (Walter Tracy), Egiziano Black (Vincent Figgins), Meta (Erik Spiekermann), Stamp Gothic (Just van Rossum) **CONCEPT:** "The theme was 'War Against the Competition,'" says designer Nancy Yeasting. "I didn't want to focus on the negative aspects of war, so for the invitation to the event, I focused on the idea of identity: What is Brentwood Mall? What does it represent? In keeping with the theme and a matching blueprint brochure, I designed the invitation as an oversized dog tag, complete with a chain!" **INSPIRATION:** A crucial scene from *Saving Private Ryan* involving the roundup of dog tags to identify the soldiers. An oversized dog tag allowed space for text and was uniquely eye-catching. The look of the design was inspired by the graphic look and boldness of old-fashioned, large woodblock type from an issue of *U&lc*. **SPECIAL TYPE TECHNIQUES:** Yeasting manipulated the computer-set type by crumpling a laser proof, covering it with tracing paper (for a dimmer image), and then photocopying it several times to further degrade the artwork. **SPECIAL PRODUCTION TECHNIQUES:** The invitation was die-cut and scored, then hand-assembled. A metal chain finishes the dog-tag look. **SPECIAL COST-CUTTING TECHNIQUES:** The custom-sized chains were produced by one of the mall's merchants, who delivered them to the marketing department's mall offices for assembly. Silver paper stock saved an extra pass of color.

W
WASHER
159
It has been honored with its own international symbol. The nuances of hot and cold are committed to memory. It is a dependable workhorse, capable of handling everything from small to extra large loads. But despite all its mastery, the washing machine alone cannot deliver perfection. Because for that, you need the finishing touch of a dryer.
LINE SCREEN 250
W.159.1100
4C
TOYO 94 CF1042
SILVER TOUCH PLATE
EMBOSS
SCULPTED
9.8 AMPS
60 Hz
120 VOLTS
ENGRAVING
TOYO CF1042
kitchen, hrdwd
k, sec parking,
450/mo. 900sf
w kit, full bath
W/D hook-up,
$850/mo sec
e 15th.
St. No dogs

STUDIO: EAI/Atlanta, Atlanta, GA **CREATIVE DIRECTORS:** David Cannon, Phil Hamlett **DESIGNERS:** Lea Nichols, David Cannon **PHOTOGRAPHER:** Greg Slater **CLIENTS/SERVICE:** Williamson Printing and Dickson's Inc./printing **SOFTWARE:** Adobe Illustrator, QuarkXPress, Adobe Photoshop **PAPER:** Mohawk Superfine Cover and Text **COLORS:** 8 (text: 5, match; cover: Hexachrome™ printing) **PAGES:** 12 pages, French fold, bound on both sides **SIZE:** 8" x 6" (20.3cm x 15.3cm) (folded); 8" x 25" (20.3cm x 63.4cm) (unfolded) **PRINT RUN:** 7,500 **TYPEFACES:** Helvetica Neue, Clarendon **INSPIRATION:** "Those modern-day wonders of the washroom: the washer and dryer combination," say the designers. **CONCEPT:** "To portray the strategic alliance of Williamson Printing, a high-quality web and sheet-fed printer, and Dickson's, a specialty printer/engraver, as the perfect combination of resources, likening the alliance to the alluring tango of the washer/dryer." **SPECIAL PRODUCTION TECHNIQUES:** Hexachrome™ printing, sculpted embossing, engraving, foil stamping, drill holes. **SPECIAL FOLDS OR FEATURES:** French fold, spiral binding.

It works its magic on the humbled wet masses. All the dryer needs is sixty minutes of quiet nurturing time and possibly some fabric softener. Fast, accurate and flexible, it handles every challenge with delicacy and finesse. Nonetheless, without the washer, the dryer would sit empty. For this is a two step process — requiring the expertise of both. In the end, even the most beastly of garments are restored to their original appealing form.

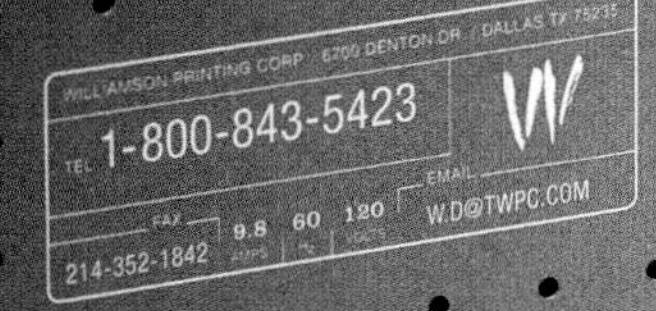

WILLIAMSON PRINTING CORP · 6700 DENTON DR / DALLAS TX 75235
TEL 1-800-843-5423
FAX
214-352-1842
9.8
AMPS
60
Hz
120
VOLTS
EMAIL
W.D@TWPC.COM

STUDIO: Visual Dialogue, Boston, MA **ART DIRECTOR:** Fritz Klaetke **DESIGNERS:** Fritz Klaetke, Carol Hayes **ILLUSTRATORS:** Bina Altera, Wade Zahares **PHOTOGRAPHERS:** John Coletti, Christopher Harting, Mark Ostow, Carl Tremblay **CLIENT/SERVICE:** Edana Spicker/artists' representative **SOFTWARE:** Adobe Photoshop, QuarkXPress **PAPER:** Strathmore Writing cover and label stock **COLORS:** 4, process **PAGES:** 1 (foldout) **SIZE:** 6" x 4 3/8" (15.3cm x 11.1cm) (folded); 6" x 36 1/2" (15.3cm x 92.7cm) (unfolded) **PRINT RUN:** 3,000 **COST PER UNIT:** US$2.50 **TYPEFACE:** Franko Old Style **CONCEPT:** "This promotional mailer for an artists' representative presents the work of her clients, as well as announcing her new address, phone number, Web site and photographer," says designer Fritz Klaetke. "It is designed to be used as a foldout brochure to present the artists as a group or, when separated at the perforations, as individual postcards." **SPECIAL TYPE TECHNIQUE:** "The type was created by my father, Frank Klaetke, on his old office typewriter." **SPECIAL PRODUCTION TECHNIQUES:** Pinhole perforation and label closure. **SPECIAL FEATURES:** Postcards are detachable.

STUDIO: Visual Dialogue, Boston, MA **ART DIRECTOR:** Fritz Klaetke **DESIGNERS:** Fritz Klaetke, Carol Hayes **ILLUSTRATORS:** Bina Altera, Wade Zahares **PHOTOGRAPHERS:** John Coletti, Christopher Harting, Mark Ostow, Carl Tremblay **CLIENT/SERVICE:** Edana Spicker/artists' representative **SOFTWARE:** Adobe Photoshop, QuarkXPress **PAPER:** Strathmore Writing cover and label stock, chipboard **COLORS:** 4, process **PAGES:** 6 plus cover **SIZE:** 7" x 5 7/8" (17.8cm x 15cm) **PRINT RUN:** 2,000 **COST PER UNIT:** US$1.50 **TYPEFACE:** Franko Old Style **CONCEPT:** "This promotional mailer for an artists' representative presents the work of her clients, as well as announcing her new Web site," says designer Fritz Klaetke. "It is designed to be used as a fold-out brochure to present the artists as a group or, when separated at the perforations, as individual postcards." **SPECIAL TYPE TECHNIQUES:** "The type was created by my father, Frank Klaetke, on his old office typewriter." **SPECIAL PRODUCTION TECHNIQUES:** Pinhole perforation (which allows postcards to be detached easily) and label closure.

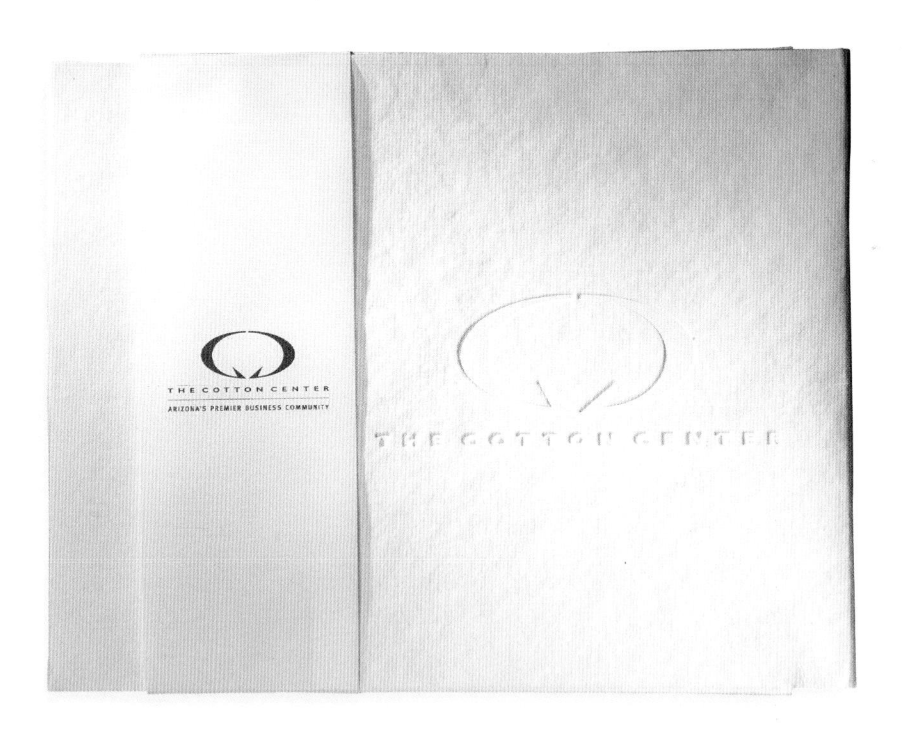

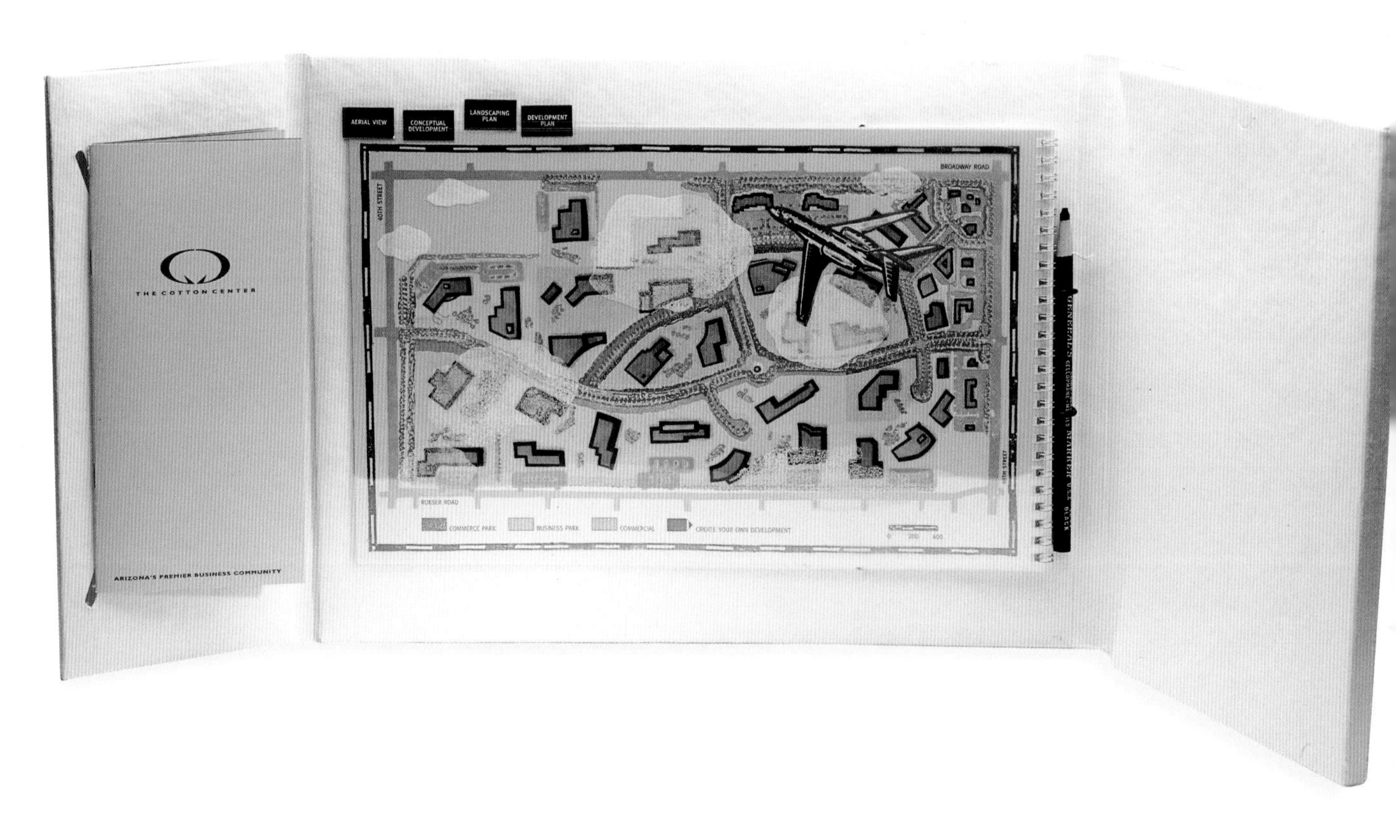

STUDIO: After Hours Creative, Phoenix, AZ **ART DIRECTOR/DESIGNER:** After Hours Creative **ILLUSTRATOR:** Rick Allen **CLIENT/PRODUCT:** The Cotton Center/commercial real estate development **SOFTWARE:** QuarkXPress, Adobe Illustrator **PAPER:** Handmade cotton rag **COLORS:** 8, match **SIZE:** 11 ½" x 15 ¼" (29.2cm x 43.9cm)(folder, shut); 8 ½" x 4" (21.6cm x 10.1cm)(pamphlet) **PRINT RUN:** 500 **TYPEFACE:** Gill Sans **INSPIRATION:** "To build on the cotton farming/agricultural heritage of the property," say the designers. **CONCEPT:** "Create your own development." Acetate flaps show the undeveloped land, landscaping plan and conceptual plan, allowing potential developers to make their own plans using a china marker. **SPECIAL FEATURES:** Acetate overlays, a china marker bound in with rubber gaskets, a UV bellyband and die-cut cotton paper folded to form a box with pocket folders. The logo is debossed on the cover, and a die-cut slit holds a project brochure.

STUDIO: Planet Design Company, Madison, WI **ART DIRECTOR:** Dana Lytle **DESIGNERS:** Ben Hirby, Dana Lytle **ILLUSTRATORS:** Lin Wilson, David Plunkert, Mark Fredrickson **COPYWRITER:** John Besmer **PHOTOGRAPHERS:** Pier Nicola D'Amico, Frederik Broden, Mark Salisbury, Michael Furman **CLIENT:** Mohawk Paper Mills, Inc. **SOFTWARE:** QuarkXPress, Adobe Illustrator, Adobe Photoshop, Macromedia Fontographer **PAPER:** Mohawk Vellum and Satin **COLORS:** Varies: 2, match metallic silver plus dull varnish; 4, process plus dull varnish; 6, match **PAGES:** 16 **SIZE:** 12" x 10" (30.5cm x 25.5cm) **TYPEFACES:** Braille Bold, Braille Oblique, Times Up, Bad Fax, Mr. Fuzzy, Punky Wunky (all by Fluff Foundry) **INSPIRATION:** "A 'This Is Spinal Tap' approach to paper promotions: an affectionate look at a genre that has more than its share of over-the-top efforts," say the designers. "The target: designers, a cynical bunch who've seen one too many pretty paper promos. This piece was a chance to have some cake and eat it too, offering silly high-concept images and overblown copy as a stark contrast to Mohawk's practical, no-nonsense approach to their Vellum and Satin line of papers. Even paper promotion standards such as production specs and printing techniques weren't spared in this effort to turn paper promotion up to an 11." **CONCEPT:** "A parody of a paper promotion." **SPECIAL PRODUCTION TECHNIQUES:** Die-cuts, quilt batting inserted in cover, rivet binding, embossing, spot color enhancement of four-color photos. **SPECIAL FOLDS:** French folds and gatefolds.

a wee bairn
was born on this day
who will e'er be known as:
Michael
FINN
Flaherty

STUDIO: EAI/Atlanta, Atlanta, GA **CREATIVE DIRECTOR:** Matt Rollins **DESIGNER:** Rebecca D'Attilio **CLIENT/SERVICE:** Martin and Lisa Flaherty/printing **SOFTWARE:** QuarkXPress **PAPER:** Astro Parche White Text **COLORS:** 4, process plus 1, match (letterpress) **PAGES:** 16 **SIZE:** 5" x 4¼" (12.7cm x 10.8cm) **PRINT RUN:** 200 **COST PER UNIT:** US$15.89 **TYPEFACE:** Poliphilus Roman **INSPIRATION:** "Robert Burns poetry and lead type." **CONCEPT:** "An Irish family announces the birth of their first son with Gaelic phraseology." **SPECIAL TYPE TECHNIQUES:** "Baseline was randomly adjusted to mimic the look of lead type," says the designer. **SPECIAL PRODUCTION TECHNIQUES:** Letterpress combined with four-color printing; stitched binding. **SPECIAL FOLDS OR FEATURES:** "A French fold was used to conceal bruises; patterns were printed on the interiors."

STUDIO: Stojan, Slovenia **DESIGNER:** Jure Stojan **CLIENT:** Self **SOFTWARE:** CorelDRAW, Macromedia Fontographer **COLORS:** 2, match **PAGES:** 4 **SIZE:** 6" x 4" (15cm x 10.1cm) (folded); 6" x 13⅞" (15cm x 35.1cm)(unfolded) **PRINT RUN:** 1,000 **TYPEFACES:** ST Raj Regular and Italic (body); ST Pekel Regular and Italic, ST Pekel Ornaments, ST Minima Regular and Italic, ST Lorn Regular and Italic, ST Vingt, ST Jure (throughout) **INSPIRATION:** "The good old envelope," says designer Jure Stojan. **CONCEPT:** A mailer for a type foundry. "The project started with very limited funds and with a serious need for effective promotion," says Stojan. "We had to economize with virtually everything. The goal was to save as much money as possible and, at the same time, to save our brochure from landing in the dustbin too quickly. Eventually we found out that the mailing represented the largest expense. We considerably lowered the costs by designing a booklet that doubles, when completely folded, as an envelope. The unfolded brochure includes the game 'Discover Our Type,' the presentation of our latest typeface release, and an order form." **SPECIAL FEATURES:** The complex piece reveals several messages when unfolded different ways, displaying previous typeface releases as well as showcasing a new one.

STUDIO: Inox Design, Milan, Italy **ART DIRECTOR:** Mauro Pastore **DESIGNER:** Claudio Gavazzi **PHOTOGRAPHER:** Lorenzo Scaccini **CLIENT:** Zanders Paper Mill **SOFTWARE:** QuarkXPress, Adobe Illustrator **PAPER:** Various Zanders papers **COLORS:** 4, process plus 1, match **PAGES:** 12 **SIZE:** 11¾" x 7½" (top edge) x 4¾" (bottom edge) (29.7cm x 19.2cm [top edge] x 12.1cm [bottom edge]) **PRINT RUN:** 8,000 **INSPIRATION:** A bouquet of flowers. **CONCEPT:** Each page is a different Zanders paper, printed with a different flower. The result is a paper bouquet. **SPECIAL PRODUCTION TECHNIQUES:** The paper sample book is cut in the shape of a bouquet of flowers. Each flower has its own die-cut. A fold on the cover sheet hides the spiral binding, keeping most of the wire inside the piece (which makes it less likely to bend, as well as more attractive). On the final page, type marks a bee's meandering passage over a specially folded, perforated response card.

STUDIO: Sibley Peteet Design, Dallas, TX **ART DIRECTOR:** Tom Hough **DESIGNER:** Tom Hough **ILLUSTRATORS:** Paul Rogers; various labels and archival materials **PHOTOGRAPHER:** Dick Patrick **CLIENT/SERVICE:** Color Dynamics/pre-press and printing **SOFTWARE:** Adobe Photoshop, Adobe Illustrator, QuarkXPress **COLORS:** 3, match (flysheet); 4, process plus 2 varnishes (interior pages and cover); 4, process (cover tip-ons) **PAGES:** 16 **SIZE:** 6¼" x 6¼" (15.8cm x 15.8cm) **TYPEFACES:** Campanula, Joanna **INSPIRATION:** Summer and all that it entails inspired this printing brochure, according to art director Tom Hough. Vibrant images of a vibrant season allow the printer to show its capabilities. A variety of fine photographs and prepress techniques, such as cutouts and shadows, demonstrate print quality. **SPECIAL FOLDS OR FEATURES:** The gloss cover includes two matte tip-ons, showcasing photography reproduction, and both sides fold in to show vintage packaging labels. Paper short sheets bound into the glossy book imitate vintage matchbooks, postcards and other memorabilia, demonstrating printing precision with spot colors.

STUDIO: Visual Asylum, San Diego, CA **ART DIRECTORS:** MaeLin Levine, Amy Jo Levine **DESIGNER:** Nicole Schlueter **ILLUSTRATOR:** Dan Renner **PHOTOGRAPHER:** Jim Coit **COPYWRITER:** Jennifer Mallory **CLIENT:** American Institute of Architects **SOFTWARE:** QuarkXPress, Adobe Illustrator **PAPER:** Carolina **COLORS:** 6, process plus UV coating **SIZE:** 7¾" x 6½" (19.7cm x 16.5cm) **PRINT RUN:** 4,200 **TYPEFACE:** Futura **INSPIRATION:** "The human scale of the built environment." **CONCEPT:** According to art director MaeLin Levine, the principal idea behind this invitation for an annual gathering of architects was a third dimension. "To create the sense of the built environment, we wanted the invitation brochure to take on a 3-D form. The San Diego environment is built from elements found in the area: water, existing architecture, art, culture and, most importantly, the human element. The viewer receives the piece flattened and is invited to pop it into the 'shadow box' form." **SPECIAL PRODUCTION TECHNIQUES:** "The piece was printed, scored, glued and laminated, then mailed flat." **SPECIAL FEATURE:** The invitation "pops" into a shadow box.

STUDIO: Visual Asylum, San Diego, CA **ART DIRECTORS:** MaeLin Levine, Amy Jo Levine **DESIGNER:** Joel Sotelo **COPYWRITER:** Troy Viss **CLIENT:** American Institute of Architects **SOFTWARE:** QuarkXPress, Adobe Illustrator **PAPER:** Utopia Premium Blue White Gloss **COLORS:** 4, process **PAGES:** 9 **SIZE:** 10" x 7" (25.4cm x 17.8cm) **PRINT RUN:** 5,000 **TYPEFACE:** Suburban **INSPIRATION:** Orchids & Onions is an annual gathering of architects and other designers concerned with development in San Diego. "The built environment is constructed from various contributors," says art director MaeLin Levine. "In this piece, a symbolic bolt and wing nut design holds them all together." **CONCEPT:** "To communicate the idea of the strength of individual design disciplines coming together to create a better community. An emphasis on architecture, interior design, urban planning, landscape architecture, graphic design." **SPECIAL PRODUCTION/COST-SAVING TECHNIQUES:** "All pieces were ganged to run together, then drilled through and hand-assembled." **SPECIAL FEATURES:** Small, irregularly shaped sheets are bolted to a larger, folded sheet that can also be used as a poster.

STUDIO: John Brady Design Consultants Inc., Pittsburgh, PA **ART DIRECTOR:** John J. Brady **DESIGNER:** Jim Bolander **ILLUSTRATOR:** Jim Bolander **PHOTOGRAPHERS:** JBDC Digital, stock, client-supplied **CLIENT:** Greater Pittsburgh Council Boy Scouts of America **SOFTWARE:** QuarkXPress, Adobe Illustrator, Adobe Photoshop **PAPER:** Fox River Rubicon Bright White Smooth Cover **COLORS:** 4, process **PAGES:** 16 plus 6 single-sheet inserts **SIZE:** 12" x 9" (30.5cm x 22.9cm) **PRINT RUN:** 1,500 **COST PER UNIT:** US$4.50 **TYPEFACES:** Adobe Garamond (body); Gill Sans (headlines); ITC Officina Sans (mission statement) **CONCEPT:** "With a limited budget, we needed to rely on special techniques that could be accomplished through volunteer labor," says art director John J. Brady. "Much of the personality was achieved by using these special collating and binding techniques." **SPECIAL PRODUCTION TECHNIQUES:** "The binding technique allowed for many different inserts to be placed throughout the text. Each page was hinge-scored and trimmed to size, and the cover was hinged- and box-scored. This allowed us to hand-bind the final books. The newspaper article was photocopied onto newsprint and torn by hand. The brown paper bag was rubber-stamped by hand. The financials were hand-written and photocopied onto actual ledger paper. Standard office supply metal fasteners were used to bind the book, and a self-adhesive metal plate (industrial supply) was placed on the front of each cover. Each plate was individually numbered." **SPECIAL COST-CUTTING TECHNIQUES:** Digital photography as well as "scanography" was used to create all the photographic images. This approach helped make the book environmentally friendly by eliminating some of the chemicals used for photo processing, and also kept the production cost down. Full-color printing had to be limited to a small number of pages due to budget. These pages were augmented with additional items, such as letters and paper bags, bound into the book to tell some of the story.

GREATER
PITTSBURGH
COUNCIL
BOY SCOUTS OF
AMERICA
1997 ANNUAL
REPORT

While the word "celebrate" has several meanings, two seem
appropriate in reflecting the year just completed by the Greater
Pittsburgh Council: 1. to commemorate with ceremony or festivity
2. to honor publicly. The pages of this report will reflect the signifi-
Celebrate
cant accomplishments made by our almost 45,000 youth members.
It is those youth who we celebrate. And we publicly honor our 10,000
volunteers for without whose time, treasures and talents
those accomplishments would not have been possible.

STUDIO: John Brady Design Consultants Inc., Pittsburgh, PA **ART DIRECTOR:** John J. Brady **DESIGNER:** Rick Madison **PHOTOGRAPHERS:** JBDC Digital, client-supplied, stock **CLIENT:** Greater Pittsburgh Council, Boy Scouts of America **SOFTWARE:** QuarkXPress, Adobe Photoshop, Adobe Illustrator **PAPER:** Fox River Confetti Sand Text and Yellow Text, Curtis Corduroy Ivy Green **COLORS:** Black only (24 pages); 4, process (12 pages) **PAGES:** 36 plus cover **SIZE:** 7" x 7" (17.8cm x 17.8cm) **PRINT RUN:** 1,000 **COST PER UNIT:** US$4 **TYPEFACES:** Adobe Garamond, Helvetica Black, Helvetica Regular **INSPIRATION:** "The great year and accomplishments of the Greater Pittsburgh Council," says art director John J. Brady. **CONCEPT:** "The Council had just completed one of their most successful years and there seemed to be cause for some celebration. The word 'Celebration' led to our concept. In addition to opening with the word, we decided to punch holes through the report and use the pieces as confetti. The confetti was attached to the front of each report in a small clear plastic bag. This allowed each recipient to 'celebrate' along with the council." **SPECIAL PRODUCTION TECHNIQUES:** "Standard three-hole punching was used to create the confetti holes on each page. Parallel wire binding allowed mixed stocks to be bound together in the proper page sequence." **SPECIAL FOLDS:** "A double gatefold in the center allowed us to create a lot of impact for the year-in-review visuals." **SPECIAL COST-CUTTING TECHNIQUES:** "Four-color printing was restricted to the center spread to maximize effect and minimize expense. Hand application of bags on the front cover eliminated the need to print on the e-flute cover stock."

STUDIO: Design Guys, Minneapolis, MN **ART DIRECTOR:** Steven Sikora **DESIGNER:** Jay Theige **PHOTOGRAPHER:** Mark Tighe **CLIENT:** AIGA Minnesota **SOFTWARE:** QuarkXPress, Adobe Illustrator **PAPER:** Potlatch McCoy Velour Text **COLORS:** 2, match **SIZE:** 10" x 5¾" (25.2cm x 14.6cm) (folded); 10" x 28¾" (25.2cm x 73cm) (unfolded) **PRINT RUN:** 1,000 **COST PER UNIT:** free **TYPEFACES:** Franklin Gothic, Adobe Garamond **INSPIRATION:** "The inspiration for the design was to shake up the status quo of AIGA newsletter design," say the Design Guys. "It is a publication for designers, for cryin' out loud!" **CONCEPT:** "Our objective was twofold: 1) do more conceptual things with the newsletter during the six months we would be responsible for it. We tried to find themes and associated secondary print processes to enhance the physical quality of the pieces. 2) Make the thing legible. We were getting pretty sick of newsletters that were illegible in the name of design." **SPECIAL TYPE TECHNIQUES:** The designers ran headline words together with color breaks "in a sort of revisited 1970s way." **SPECIAL PRODUCTION TECHNIQUES:** For each issue the Design Guys specified a different second printing process. Because the work was donated, things didn't always work out as planned—as was the case with this issue. It was supposed to feature laser die-cutting, with round, punched-out holes spelling the word "Issues" through the entire folded newsletter. "The vendor backed out and offered us a clear sparkle screen-printing process instead," the Design Guys say. "We went with it, overprinting the big fish on the cover and subtly printing the word in place of the die-cut." **SPECIAL FOLDS OR FEATURES:** The ten-panel, accordion-folded piece is printed on both sides. **SPECIAL COST-CUTTING TECHNIQUES:** Free printing in return for credit.

STUDIO: Kan & Lau Design Consultants, Hong Kong, China **ART DIRECTORS:** Kan Tai-keung, Eddy Yu Chi Kong **DESIGNERS:** Kan Tai-keung, Eddy Yu, Benson Kwun, Leung Wai Yin **COMPUTER ILLUSTRATORS:** Benson Kwun, John Tam, Leung Wai Yin **CHINESE INK ILLUSTRATIONS:** Kan Tai-keung **PHOTOGRAPHER:** C.K. Wong **CHINESE CALLIGRAPHY:** Yip Man-Yam, Chui Tze-Hung, Yung Ho-Yin **SEAL ENGRAVING:** Yip Man-Yam **CLIENT:** Tokushu Paper Manufacturing Co. Ltd. **SOFTWARE:** Macromedia FreeHand, Adobe Photoshop, Live Picture **PAPER:** Bornfree Recycled Paper Warm White, Enamel Green, Charcoal, Red Dates, China Red, Beige **COLORS:** 4, process plus several match colors and colored foils **PAGES:** 19 **SIZE:** 9¾" x 7" (24.7cm x 17.7cm) **ENGLISH TYPEFACE:** Adobe Garamond **CHINESE TYPEFACES:** Monotype MSung Light and Medium; Dyna DEFang Song **CONCEPT:** Designed for the Chinese market, the papers in this swatch book mimic the feel and bamboo-grained surface of traditional Chinese handmade papers. Chinese imagery and calligraphy provide the design elements, while elaborate printing techniques show what the paper can do. **SPECIAL TYPE TECHNIQUES:** Chinese ink illustration and calligraphy. **SPECIAL PRODUCTION TECHNIQUES:** Engraving, hot stamping, varnish, die-cutting and embossing.

STUDIO: Mindconcept Design, Hong Kong, China **ART DIRECTOR/DESIGNER:** Chui Tak Ming (John) **ILLUSTRATOR:** Chan Ka Wai (David) **PHOTOGRAPHER:** Yueng Kam Ming **CLIENT:** Self **SOFTWARE:** Adobe Photoshop, Macromedia FreeHand **PAPER:** Hi-Born HK **COLORS:** 2, match **SIZE:** 4" x 12 ¼" (10cm x 31cm)(unfolded) **PRINT RUN:** 500 **COST PER UNIT:** US$1.92 **TYPEFACES:** MSung Medium (Chinese text); custom (Chinese characters on upper right-hand corner); Triplex Bold (English text); Triplex Serif Bold (English text) **INSPIRATION:** Between 1998 and 1999 the economies of Hong Kong and Macau were in recession. This calendar was designed to encourage people to march forward to the coming year to make it more prosperous. **CONCEPT:** The ship depicted on the calendar is a well-equipped ship rather than a warship; its strength and provisions can withstand the difficult conditions, allowing the ship to progress forward. **SPECIAL FEATURES:** Embossing. **SPECIAL COST-CUTTING TECHNIQUES:** The die-cutting was done after the pieces were embossed.

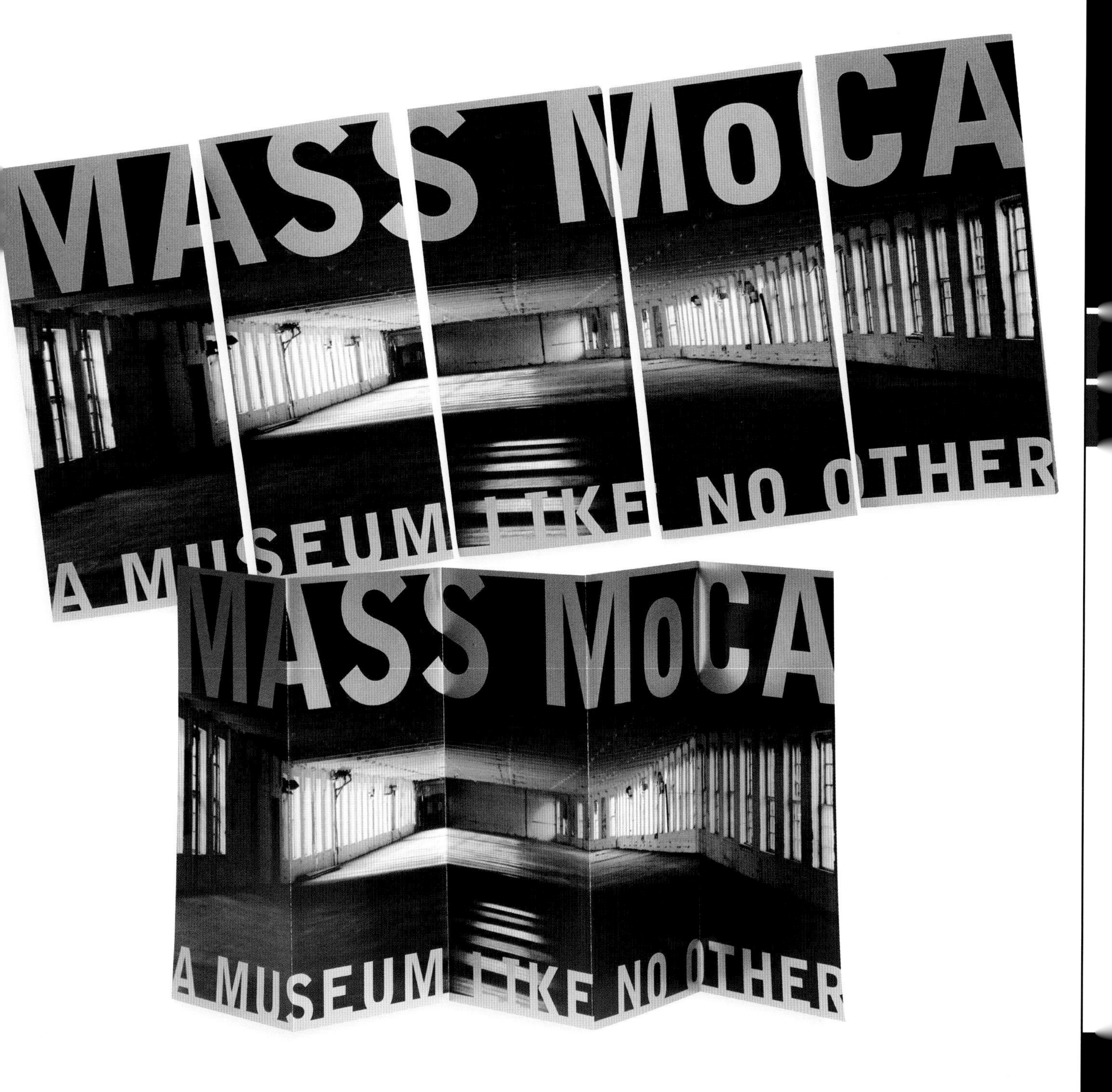

STUDIO: Massachusetts Museum of Contemporary Art Design Department, North Adams, MA **ART DIRECTOR/DESIGNER:** Doug Bartow **PHOTOGRAPHER:** Nicholas Whitman **CLIENT:** Massachusetts Museum of Contemporary Art (MASS MoCA) **SOFTWARE:** Adobe Photoshop, QuarkXPress, Adobe Illustrator **PAPER:** Opus Dull Text **COLORS:** 4, process plus match metallic silver and 1, match **SIZE:** 9" x 4" (22.9cm x 10.2cm) (folded); 9" x 20" (22.9cm x 50.8cm) (unfolded) **PRINT RUN:** 50,000 **COST PER UNIT:** US$0.10 **TYPEFACE:** Bell Gothic (M. Carter)
CONCEPT: The inspiration, according to designer Doug Bartow, was a blueprint or working model of the art center, which was set to open in two years. Photographs and text are set on top of a line drawing of the twenty-seven-building site that once housed a mill, allowing people to understand its scale. **SPECIAL PRODUCTION TECHNIQUES:** To achieve the solid silver, the printer overprinted it on top of black. **SPECIAL FOLDS OR FEATURES:** The printer accordion-folded the piece five different ways, so that the brochures can be displayed in groups of five that reveal the foldout image.

STUDIO: Visual Asylum, San Diego, CA **ART DIRECTORS:** MaeLin Levine, Amy Jo Levine **DESIGNER:** Christine Drashner **CLIENT/PRODUCT:** Nexo/footwear **SOFTWARE:** Adobe Illustrator **COLORS:** Black plus varnish **PAGES:** 2 (3 printed sides) **SIZE:** 4½" x 4½" (11.4cm x 11.4cm)(folded); 9" x 9" (22.9cm x 22.9cm)(unfolded) **TYPEFACE:** Rockwell **CONCEPT:** "To create a quick give-away brochure that was intriguing and a quick read for an upcoming trade show," says art director MaeLin Levine. **SPECIAL TYPE TECHNIQUES:** "The product price list was printed on a translucent vellum sheet and designed to reveal the typography beneath. The two pieces layer to create a rich texture of typography." **SPECIAL FOLDS:** "The piece folds in half and then in half again, with diagonal folds to create interesting copy-block shapes. This was done to reinforce the logotype's strong vertical, horizontal and diagonal shapes."

STUDIO: Visual Asylum, San Diego, CA **ART DIRECTORS:** MaeLin Levine, Amy Jo Levine **DESIGNER:** Charles Glaubitz **ILLUSTRATOR:** Charles Glaubitz **CLIENT:** American Institute of Graphic Arts, San Diego **SOFTWARE:** QuarkXPress, Adobe Illustrator **COLORS:** 4, process **PAGES:** 1 **SIZE:** 3" x 3" (7.6cm x 7.6cm) (folded); 6" x 6" (15.2cm x 15.2cm) (unfolded) **PRINT RUN:** 500 **TYPEFACE:** Futura **INSPIRATION:** "A childhood fortune-telling puzzle," says art director MaeLin Levine. **CONCEPT:** "This was created specifically for HOW Conference attendees. The top ten design firms in San Diego each made a piece recommending their top ten 'must-see' San Diego highlights. Our concept was to create something fun and interactive." **SPECIAL FOLDS:** "The piece was a perfect square, scored and folded in half, and in half again, with diagonal folds, to create the finger puzzle shape."

"What's the big idea?" one of Damon Runyan's guys might ask a doll who swipes his racing forms. This chapter asks the same question. When a big idea drives the design, you don't need a handicapper to tell you to bet on success.

[concept]

[concept] 5

in these pages, you'll see how:

- 5D Studio used CAD drawings to promote a product that hadn't been built yet—creating a flip book to show how a chair based on shopping cart design nests with its mates and rolls into storage.
- Designer Pat Taylor commissioned his friends and colleagues to create one-page pieces in honor of his thirtieth business anniversary, and printed them as a promotional book.
- A company name (Fierce) and product (leather belts and other items) led Beehive Design to envision a secret laboratory breeding dangerously feral leather.

STUDIO: CookSherman, San Francisco, CA **ART DIRECTOR:** Ken Cook **DESIGNER:** Ken Cook **PHOTOGRAPHER:** Hunter Freeman Studio **CLIENT/SERVICE:** Hunter Freeman Studio/photography **SOFTWARE:** QuarkXPress, Adobe Illustrator, Adobe Photoshop **PAPER:** Potlatch Quintessence Gloss Cover **COLORS:** 4, process plus 2, match and spot dull and gloss varnishes **PAGES:** 10 **SIZE:** 12½" x 9¼" (31.6cm x 23.5cm) **PRINT RUN:** 5,000 **COST PER UNIT:** US$12 **TYPEFACES:** Hadriano (cover); Copperplate, Stempel Garamond, Shelley **CONCEPT:** "To promote car photography by using metal material for the brochure cover," says designer Ken Cook. **SPECIAL PRODUCTION TECHNIQUES:** The embossed metal cover is spiral-bound, and includes a glued-on toy license plate. **SPECIAL FOLDS:** A 36-inch sheet of horizontal paper, printed on both sides with giant-sized car photos, is accordion-folded into the piece.

concept

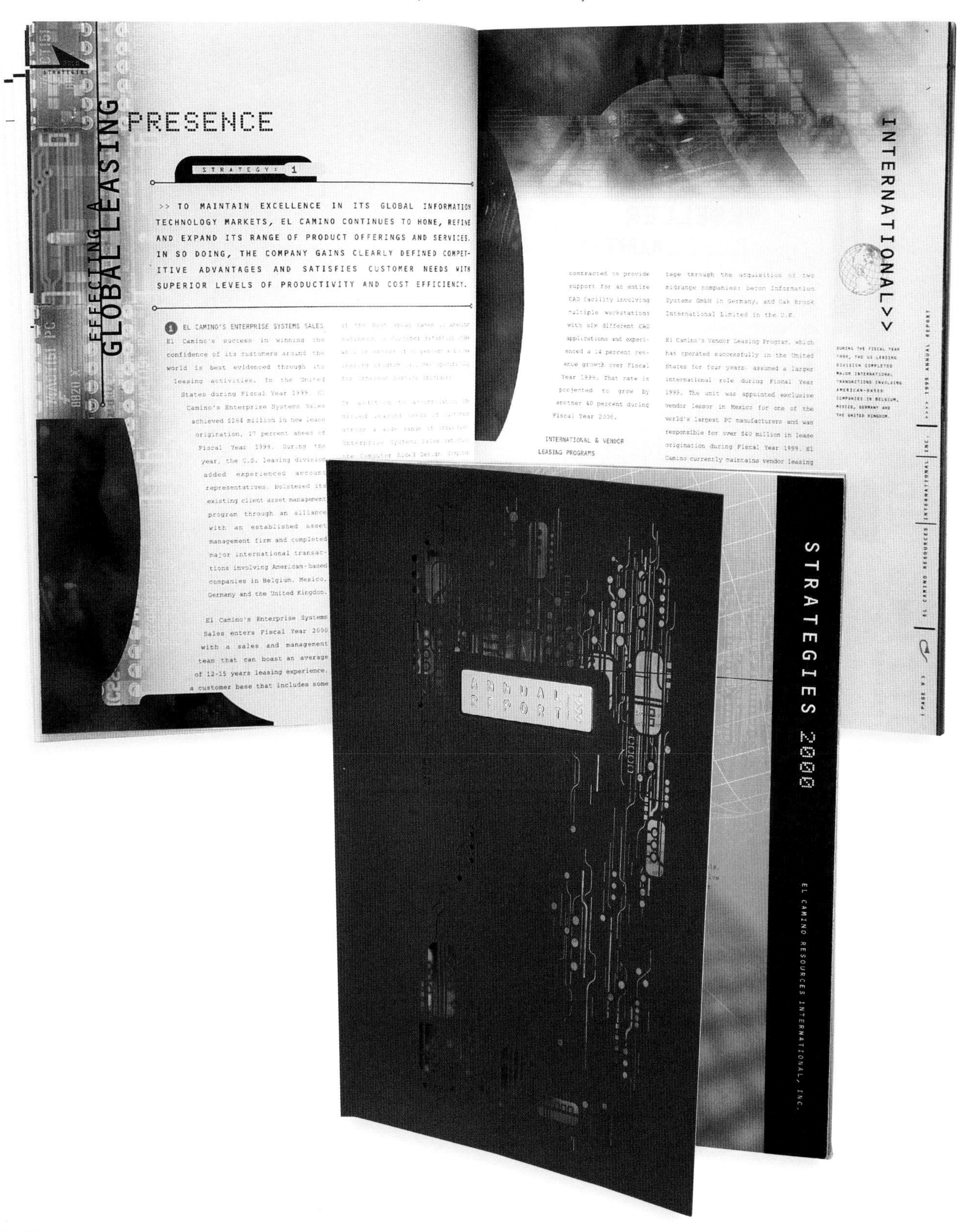

STUDIO: [i]e design, Studio City, CA **ART DIRECTOR:** Marcie Carson **DESIGNER:** Cya Nelson **PHOTOGRAPHY:** Stock CD (manipulated) **CLIENT/SERVICE:** El Camino Resources International, Inc./computer mainframe reseller, lessor; information technology solution provider and electronic commerce developer **SOFTWARE:** Adobe Photoshop, Adobe Illustrator, QuarkXPress **PAPER:** Mohawk Options (cover); CTI Glama Opaline (interior); Strathmore Elements, Grid (financials) **COLORS:** 4, process plus black **PAGES:** 38 plus cover **SIZE:** 11¾" x 9" (29.8cm x 22.8cm) **PRINT RUN:** 6,000 (English); 2,500 (Spanish); 1,000 (Portuguese) **COST PER UNIT:** US$18.25 **TYPEFACES:** Courier (body copy); OCR-B (subheads, folios); Bubbledot ICG (heads) **INSPIRATION:** Circuitry. **CONCEPT:** "We wanted to visually depict the inner workings of a computer—its thoughts, communication and movement," says art director Marcie Carson. "This concept led to the circuit board pattern that was laser-cut into the cover; it invites the reader inside the workings of the annual. We decided to print the computer-driven design on French-folded vellum sheets so that the layout was constantly changing and moving, much like a computer." **SPECIAL PRODUCTION TECHNIQUES:** Four-color process was printed full-coverage on vellum, which is more difficult than it appears. All type was printed in a fifth color, black; this way English, Spanish and Portuguese versions of the text could be done in three separate print runs. **SPECIAL FEATURES:** Laser-cut circuit board pattern and the embossed metal plate tip-in on the cover. For the French-folded pages, the design was printed on only one side of the sheet, and the outer edge was folded; the inner edge was perfect-bound. **SPECIAL COST-CUTTING TECHNIQUES:** Numerous CD-ROM stock photographs were collaged with illustrations done by the studio to create "custom" computer imagery. This way the money allocated for the photography budget could be put into the printing.

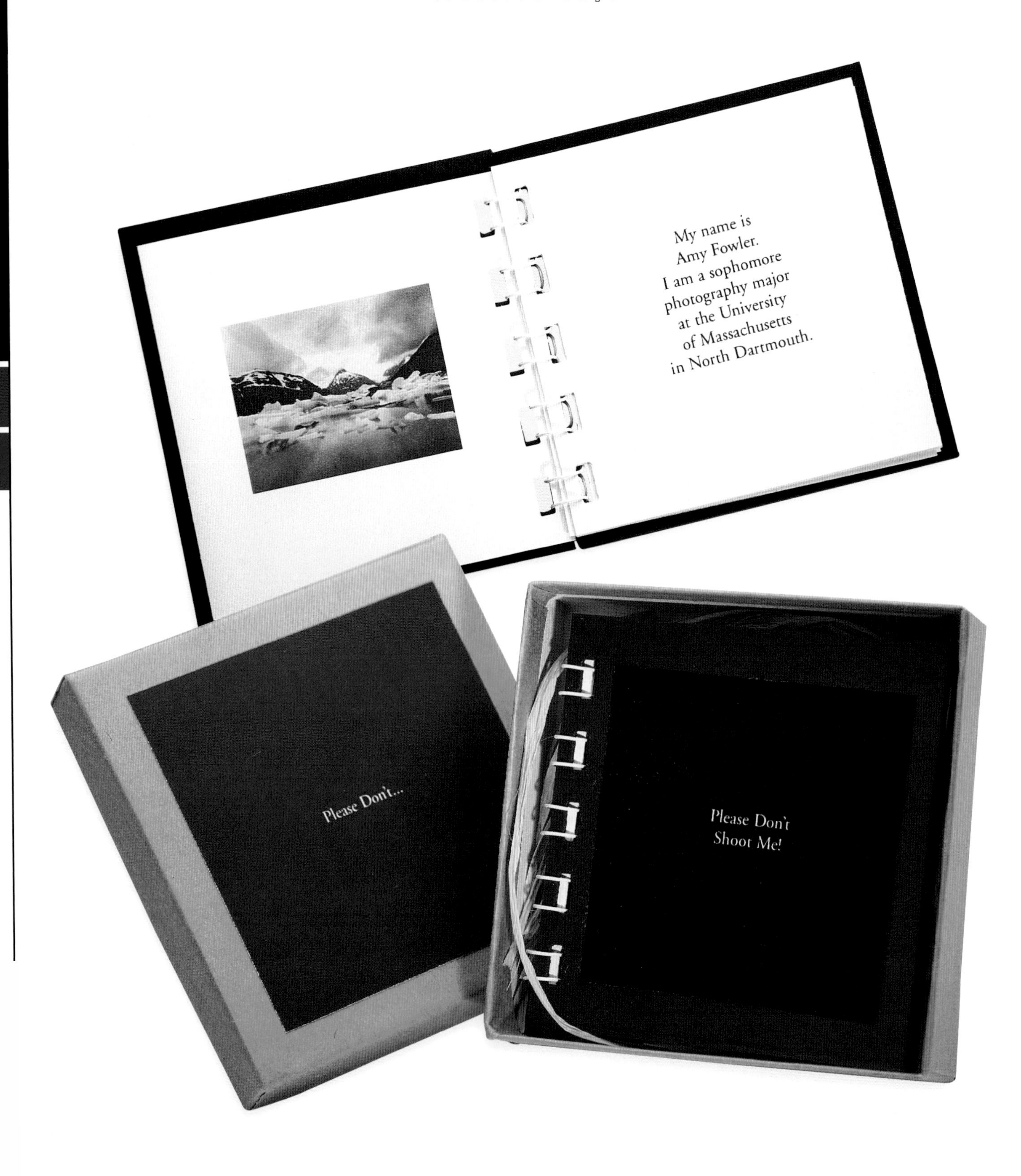

My name is
Amy Fowler.
I am a sophomore
photography major
at the University
of Massachusetts
in North Dartmouth.
Please Don't...
Please Don't
Shoot Me!

STUDIO: Tom Fowler, Inc., Stamford, CT **ART DIRECTOR/DESIGNER:** Amy Fowler **PHOTOGRAPHER:** Amy Fowler **CLIENT/SERVICE:** Amy Fowler/student photography assistant **SOFTWARE:** QuarkXPress, Adobe Photoshop **PAPER:** Hammermill Bond **COLORS:** Black **PAGES:** 10 **SIZE:** 3 ¼" x 3 ¼" (8.3cm x 8.3cm) (book); 3 11/16" x 3 11/16" (9.3cm x 9.3cm) (box) **PRINT RUN:** 30 **COST PER UNIT:** US$7 **TYPEFACE:** Adobe Garamond **INSPIRATION:** "A college student's need for a summer job," says college student Amy Fowler. **CONCEPT:** "To pull the viewer into the piece and keep him/her interested by including a sample of photographs from my portfolio." **SPECIAL PRODUCTION TECHNIQUES:** "I used a wood punch to engrave my initials into the back cover." **SPECIAL COST-CUTTING TECHNIQUES:** "Because of the limited number of promotions in this set, I was able to produce and assemble each piece by hand."

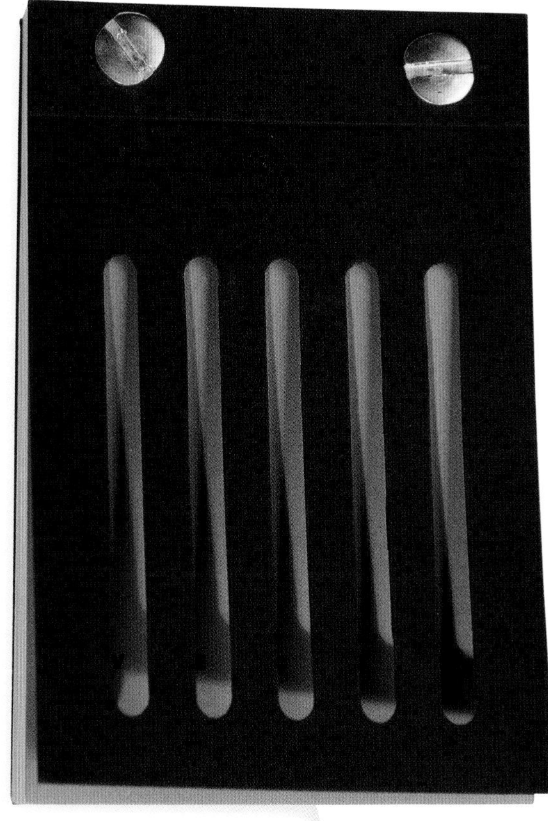

STUDIO: 5D Studio, Malibu, CA **ART DIRECTOR:** Jane Kobayashi **DESIGNER:** Geoff Ledet **ILLUSTRATOR:** IDEO **PHOTOGRAPHER:** Elyn Marton **CLIENT/PRODUCT:** Vecta/contract furniture **SOFTWARE:** Adobe Photoshop, QuarkXPress (CAD drawings were provided) **PAPER:** Fox River Quest Black Cover Plus (cover); DaiEi Topkote White Cover Gloss (text) **COLORS:** Black plus metallic silver **PAGES:** 60 plus cover **SIZE:** 2 ¾" x 4 ¼" (7cm x 10.8cm) **INITIAL PRINT RUN:** 10,000 (second print run: 10,000) **COST PER UNIT:** US$2.50 **TYPEFACES:** Helvetica Neue Bold and Thin **INSPIRATION:** "Vecta had an innovative product, Kart™, a special chair that could be used for training centers, seminars and conferences and compactly stored away, yet also was comfortable to sit in for hours at a time," says art director Jane Kobayashi. "The Kart™ is the only task chair that folds up and nests (like a shopping cart, thus the name). The client challenged us to design a 'memorable giveaway' for the product's introduction at NeoCon (an annual contract furniture show in Chicago). The only problem was, the actual chair did not exist yet and the prototypes would not deliver until the show." **CONCEPT:** "It was important to demonstrate how the chair swivels and nests together, as well as add a little humor. The flip book was something we could produce without the actual product. For a little tongue-in-cheek humor relating to the shopping cart concept, we added the 'box boy' at the end. The same image sequence was also made into a screensaver used in the showrooms." **SPECIAL PRODUCTION TECHNIQUES:** "Working with IDEO's CAD drawings in incremental movements, we took photographs moving in tandem with the 'box boy,' keeping in mind that we needed to match the angle and proportions of the CAD drawings. We merged the box boy and the chair in Photoshop." **SPECIAL FEATURES:** "The die-cut on the cover is taken from a design detail of the chair back. The book is held with two Chicago screws."

STUDIO: Winston-Ford Design, West Hartford, CT **ART DIRECTOR/DESIGNER:** Richard Hollant **ILLUSTRATOR:** Richard Hollant **COPYWRITER:** Richard Hollant **CLIENT:** Self **SOFTWARE:** Adobe Photoshop, Macromedia FreeHand, QuarkXPress **PAPER:** Gilbert ESSE, Smooth and Textured **COLORS:** 4, process plus 2, match **PAGES:** 12 **SIZE:** 3¾" x 8½" (9.3cm x 21.6cm) **PRINT RUN:** 1,500 **COST PER UNIT:** US$1 **TYPEFACES:** Courier, Dynamoe, Swiss, New Baskerville, Dogma, vineta, Parisian, Koloss and "some other silly, exaggerated display fonts, some of which were digitally re-rendered for special effects," says art director Richard Hollant. **INSPIRATION:** "1) Green Stamps books that my folks used to fill up obsessively, and 2) the inside back cover of DC Comics that itemized the stuff you could order." **CONCEPT:** "Here's how it works: along with the first invoice, we would include this booklet. It says 'Thanks for the work,' and includes a snazzy numbered coupon that the client can collect along with coupons accompanying subsequent invoices. The book has a series of offerings including three coupons to get X-ray glasses; a blimp bank or marching robot for five coupons; and an American-in-Paris kit full of kitschy souvenirs. We had fun. Clients had fun. They saw another side of what we do and who we are. We got to watch them play." **SPECIAL PRODUCTION TECHNIQUES:** "Mixed stocks held by Acco clasps from Staples allows us to replace pages as the items go out of stock and add new stuff whenever we get inspired. Seriously cheesy foil embossed stickers were created for the foil section. I had a seal produced, an homage to the Green Stamp roots of the piece. Finding a vendor with a pinhole wheel perforating machine was the hardest part of the project, but in the end worth the effort." **SPECIAL COST-CUTTING TECHNIQUES:** "This job was run on a sheet with four other jobs, each of which printed on a different stock. This yielded four distinct brochures with distinct feels, for just a tiny bit more than the price of one. The down side: I had to say several novenas for the wasted paper."

CAUTION:
READING THIS ANNUAL REPORT
MAY CAUSE AN ERECTION
IMPOTENCE IS
OPTIONAL
corpus cavernosum
corpus cavernosum
urethra
MUSE
corpus spongiosum
CROSS SECTION OF PENIS
artist's rendering
HOW MUSE
WORKS
TRANSURETHRAL ADMINISTRATION IS BASED ON THE DISCOVERY THAT VASCULAR COMMUNICATIONS EXIST BETWEEN THE CORPUS SPONGIOSUM AND THE CORPUS CAVERNOSUM. MUSE DELIVERS ALPROSTADIL DIRECTLY TO THE URETHRAL MUCOSA, WHERE TRANSURETHRAL ABSORPTION IS RAPID — 80% OF THE DOSE IS ABSORBED WITHIN TEN MINUTES OF APPLICATION. LOCAL ABSORPTION PROMOTES SMOOTH ARTERIAL MUSCLE RELAXATION AND MAY RESULT IN RAPID ARTERIAL BLOOD INFLOW AND PENILE RIGIDITY.

STUDIO: Cahan & Associates, San Francisco, CA **ART DIRECTOR:** Bill Cahan **DESIGNER:** Kevin Roberson **ILLUSTRATOR:** Kevin Roberson **CLIENT/SERVICE:** Vivus, Inc./impotence treatment **SOFTWARE:** QuarkXPress, Adobe Illustrator **PAPER:** Weyerhaeuser Cougar Opaque **COLORS:** 4, match **PAGES:** 36 plus cover **SIZE:** 11¾" x 9¼" (29.7cm x 23.6cm) **TYPEFACE:** Futura (Paul Renner) **INSPIRATION:** "Solely in response to the management's request," says designer Kevin Roberson. **CONCEPT:** "Vivus develops treatments for erectile dysfunction, more commonly known as impotence. Although this annual report primarily contains a straightforward business message, the use of bold diagrams, large oblique type and a stiff hard cover convey the end result of using their product." A humorous cover band gets the report's message across at a glance. **SPECIAL PRODUCTION TECHNIQUES:** Part of the production run had a hard cover; the rest used heavy cardboard.

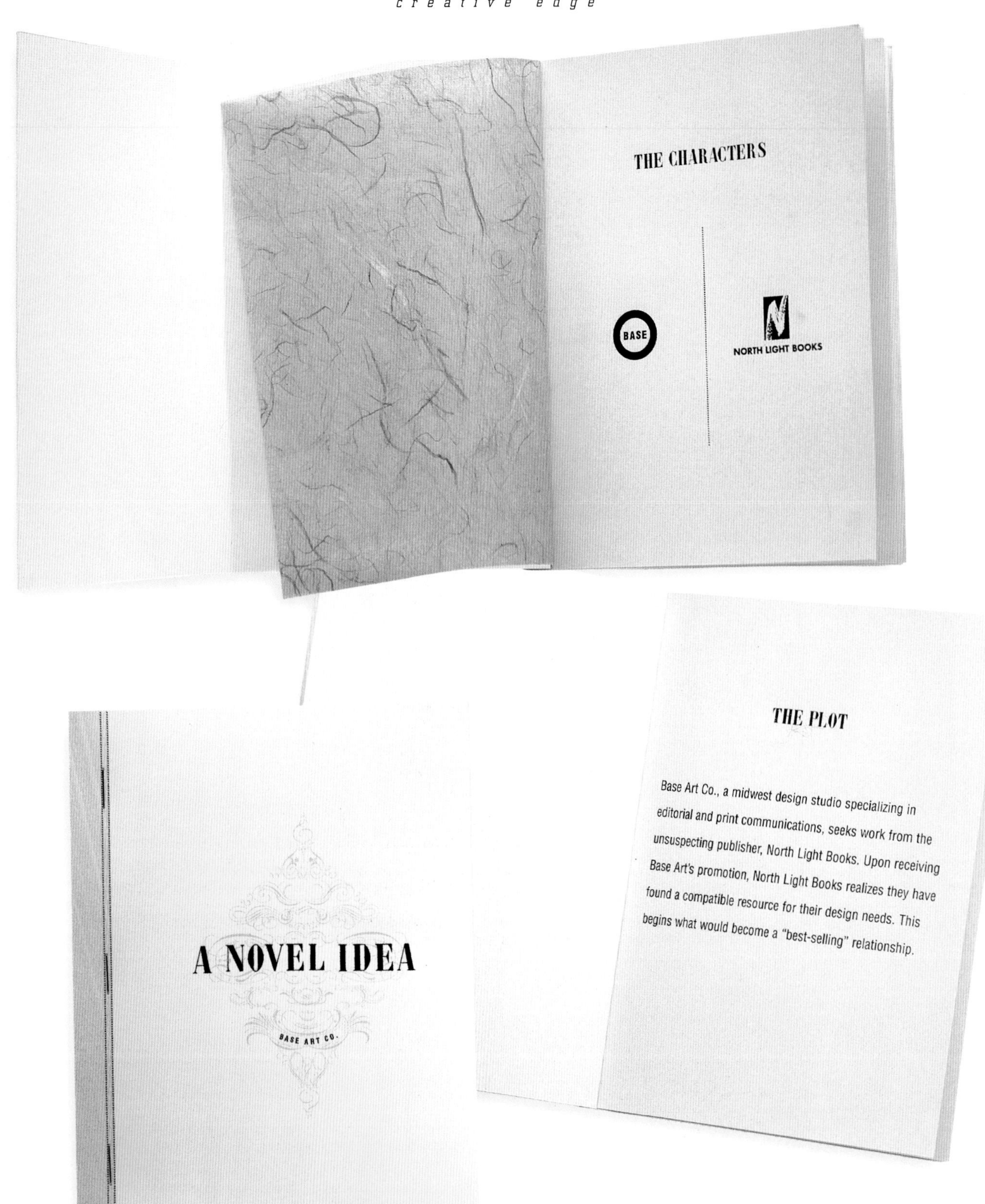

THE CHARACTERS
BASE
NORTH LIGHT BOOKS
THE PLOT
Base Art Co., a midwest design studio specializing in editorial and print communications, seeks work from the unsuspecting publisher, North Light Books. Upon receiving Base Art's promotion, North Light Books realizes they have found a compatible resource for their design needs. This begins what would become a "best-selling" relationship.
A NOVEL IDEA
BASE ART CO.

STUDIO: Base Art Co., Columbus, OH **ART DIRECTOR/DESIGNER:** Terry Alan Rohrbach **PRODUCTION ASSISTANCE:** Jesse Bulger, Columbus, OH **CLIENT:** Self **SOFTWARE:** QuarkXPress, Adobe Photoshop **PAPER:** Ink-jet compatible stock, Japanese papers, novel pages **COLORS:** Laser and ink-jet output **PAGES:** 10 **SIZE:** 6½" x 5" (16.5cm x 12.8cm) **PRINT RUN:** 200 **COST PER UNIT:** US$1 **TYPEFACES:** MGrotesque, found woodcut letters **CONCEPT:** "Wanting to expand on our jacket design niche, Base Art Co. developed this promotion as a format to showcase recent book covers produced for a variety of publishers," says designer Terry Alan Rohrbach. "Our 'soft sell' intentions were presented in a novel format, listing the characters (Base Art Co. and the potential client) and a plot based on our 'new relationship' with that client. The cover designs were tipped on actual pages from classic novels." **INSPIRATION:** "The idea came out of our frustration in drafting a cover letter. I wanted to send something that was more than just a portfolio sample. It seemed appropriate to make the vehicle a book in itself!" **SPECIAL COST-CUTTING TECHNIQUES:** "The entire piece was output in-house on laser and ink-jet printers and then hand-assembled. This kept costs down for our low production quantities and enabled us to personalize the character list for each piece."

STUDIO: Pat Taylor Inc., Washington, DC **ART DIRECTOR:** Pat Taylor **DESIGNERS:** Various **ILLUSTRATORS:** Various **PHOTOGRAPHERS:** Nancy Rayburn, Gordon Fisher **CLIENT:** Self **COLORS:** Match black **PAGES:** 32 **SIZE:** 5" x 4" (12.7cm x 10.3cm) **PRINT RUN:** 750 **COST PER UNIT:** US$1 **TYPEFACES:** Smith Corona 250 DCE plus various **INSPIRATION:** "Doodles book on Herb Lubalin's stationery by various artists and designers in the early 1960s, concept by Ernie Smith," says Pat Taylor. **CONCEPT:** "To allow each designer friend to express himself or herself with a page." **SPECIAL PRODUCTION TECHNIQUE:** "The book was put together for the printer by the old way—mechanical artboards from printouts from each designer." **SPECIAL FOLDS:** "Cover 1 + 4 folded in to make for a heavier cover." **SPECIAL COST-CUTTING TECHNIQUE:** "I used one sheet of paper for all thirty-two pages, so it went only once through the press."

STUDIO: Beehive Design, Toronto, Ontario, Canada **DESIGNER:** Terry Lau **ILLUSTRATOR:** Michael Brennan **PHOTOGRAPHER:** Angela Brown **CLIENT/PRODUCT:** Fierce Leather/leather belts and accessories **SOFTWARE:** QuarkXPress, Adobe Illustrator, Adobe Photoshop **PAPER:** Supreme Dull **COLORS:** 4, process **PAGES:** 36 plus cover **SIZE:** 6" x 9" (15.2cm x 22.8cm) **PRINT RUN:** 4,000 **TYPEFACE:** Helvetica Condensed **INSPIRATION:** Science fiction. **CONCEPT:** "Instead of a conventional product catalog," says designer Terry Lau, "the client requested a more dynamic and visually stimulating sales piece. Beehive came up with the concept that the leather being produced was genetically engineered inside this fictitious laboratory by a group of renegade scientists." **SPECIAL PRODUCTION TECHNIQUE:** Matte laminate cover. "It provided an X-ray effect."

Fashion has always been an inexact science. Until now.
The work at Fierce Laboratory centred around total synthesis of organic materials, extrapolating from base DNA. The successful creation of organic material that was identical to the original, down to the molecular level, would have countless applications. Working with leather, a relatively simple and inert organic substance, there were a series of breakthroughs. Genetic matches of 45.3%, then 78.23% and finally 98.23% were reached in rapid succession, but went no further. Fierce Laboratory's leather differed from organic leather by 1.77%, but what was most disturbing about this was that none of the scientists involved were able to locate how it was different.
The elusive 1.77%
6 normal
3 afflicted
7 normal
fig. 1) A175.iron.20
fig. 2) C150.GD.10
fig. 3) C175.iron.10
fig. 1) C125.100.10R
stainless steel buckle
english bridle leather
available in brown
fig. 2) C125.100.10S
stainless steel buckle
english bridle leather
available in brown
fig. 3) C150.100.10R
fig. 4) C150.100.10R
fig. 5) C150.RACER.BLUE
stainless steel buckle
english bridle leather
fig. 6) C150.RACER.YELLOW
stainless steel buckle
english bridle leather
fig. 1) Toni side bag
The broken DNA strand gave the substance a notable tendency to bond with the nearest organic substance, whether it be something as simple as rubber or as complex as a human being. Initial stages in exposed humans included possessiveness. Secondary stages were marked by dynamic and unusually spontaneous behaviour.

STUDIO: Wages Design, Inc., Atlanta, GA **ART DIRECTORS:** Bob Wages, Randall Allison **DESIGNER:** Randall Allison **ILLUSTRATOR:** Randall Allison **PHOTOGRAPHER:** Jerry Burns **CLIENT/SERVICE:** Cadmus Communications, PharmaC3 Division/pharmaceutical package design, printing and distribution **SOFTWARE:** QuarkXPress, Adobe Photoshop, Adobe Illustrator **COLORS:** 4, process plus 2, match **PAGES:** 16 plus cover and sleeve **SIZE:** 7 1/8" x 7" (18cm x 17.7cm)(package, folded); 6" x 6" (15.3cm x 15.3cm)(pamphlet) **TYPEFACES:** Futura, Frutiger **CONCEPT:** "To help pharmaceutical companies find a single source for their printing support," says designer Randall Allison. "Using medical, health and business images to reference the 'PharmaC3' concept (create, produce, distribute), we sought to convey Cadmus's ability to focus entirely on their customers." **SPECIAL FEATURES:** A folded paper package holds the piece. Its cover is printed with a closed eye; the recipient opens the cover to reveal an open eye. Printing techniques, including various spot varnishes, show off the client's capabilities.

WITHOUT CONTRAST,
INTERPRETING IMAGES CAN
BE A LOT OF GUESSWORK.
SEE SPOT?
WITH CONTRAST
INFORMATION IS POWER. OPTISON CONTRAST ECHO TAKES THE GUESSWORK OUT OF DIAGNOSIS.
NO THROMBUS
NORMAL THICKNESS
NORMAL MOTION
HELPING DOCTORS HELP PATIENTS OPTISON, DEVELOPED AND MANUFACTURED BY MOLECULAR BIOSYSTEMS, IS THE WORLD'S ONLY APPROVED ADVANCED-GENERATION ULTRASOUND CONTRAST AGENT. INDICATED FOR USE IN PATIENTS WITH SUBOPTIMAL ECHOCARDIOGRAMS TO ASSESS BLOOD FLOW WITHIN THE HEART CHAMBERS AND IDENTIFY THE LOCATION OF THE CHAMBER BORDERS AND THE MOVEMENT OF THE CHAMBER WALLS, OPTISON HELPS DOCTORS MAKE DIAGNOSES ACCURATELY AND CONFIDENTLY. HOW? BY HELPING THEM SEE THE ANATOMY OF THE HEART MORE CLEARLY VIA ULTRASOUND.

STUDIO: Cahan & Associates, San Francisco, CA **ART DIRECTOR:** Bill Cahan **DESIGNER:** Kevin Roberson **ILLUSTRATOR:** Kevin Roberson **PHOTOGRAPHERS:** Ken Probst, various **CLIENT/SERVICE:** Molecular Biosystems, Inc./ultrasound contrast agents **SOFTWARE:** QuarkXPress, Adobe Photoshop **PAPER:** French Dur-o-Tone Newsprint, Potlatch Vintage Velvet **COLORS:** 2, match (cover); 4, process plus 2, match (interior) **PAGES:** 44 plus cover **SIZE:** 12½" x 10⅛" (31.8cm x 25.7cm) **TYPEFACE:** Trade Gothic (Jackson Burke) **INSPIRATION:** "Late night television." **CONCEPT:** "A substantial portion of ultrasound images are unfit to be diagnosed due to poor contrast," says designer Kevin Roberson. "Molecular Biosystems has created an in vivo contrast agent which dramatically increases readability and clarity of ultrasound images. In order to capture the importance of this significant development, a series of murky photographs are presented with questions asking the reader to identify and 'diagnose' the content. This quiz-like exercise is analogous to the cardiologist's predicament of making accurate diagnoses without clear images." **SPECIAL PRODUCTION TECHNIQUES:** Special halftones replicate the look of poor-quality ultrasound images. **SPECIAL FEATURE:** A response card allows recipients to 'diagnose' the murky photos and send in their answers. Top scorers received a gift and a chance to win one hundred shares of the client's stock.

STUDIO: Campbell Fisher Ditko Design, Phoenix, AZ **ART DIRECTORS:** Steve Ditko, Mike Tomko **DESIGNERS:** Mike Tomko, Steve Ditko **ILLUSTRATORS:** Steve Ditko, Mike Tomko **PHOTOGRAPHERS:** Steve Ditko, Mike Tomko, Mike Campbell **CLIENT:** Self **SOFTWARE:** QuarkXPress, Adobe Illustrator, Adobe Photoshop, Adobe Dimensions **PAPER:** S.D. Warren Strobe Dull **COLORS:** 4, process plus 2, match **PAGES:** 66 **SIZE:** 8½" x 5½" (21.6cm x 14cm) **PRINT RUN:** 2,500 **COST PER UNIT:** US$10 ($30 retail, without tradeouts) **TYPEFACE:** Univers **INSPIRATION:** "Fine art and photography books," say the designers. **CONCEPT:** "To experiment." An array of provocative imagery and copy challenges the recipient to look at life in a new way—or call the designer to do so. **SPECIAL PRODUCTION TECHNIQUE:** The title is embossed in reverse on the cover. **SPECIAL FEATURE:** Smyth-sewn binding.

STUDIO: Seven Productions, Kontich, Belgium **ART DIRECTOR:** Sven Mastbooms **DESIGNERS:** Sven Mastbooms, Jeroen van Omme (3-D work) **ILLUSTRATORS:** Sven Mastbooms, Jeroen van Omme **CLIENT/PRODUCT:** EMI Music Belgium/record company **SOFTWARE:** Adobe Illustrator, Adobe Photoshop, Lightwave, QuarkXPress **PAPER:** Maco Satine **COLORS:** 4, process **PAGES:** 8 **SIZE:** 4¾" x 4¾" (12.1cm x 12.1cm) (folded) **TYPEFACES:** Pauline, Helvetica Neue, handwriting using Wacom tablet and pen **INSPIRATION:** "The contrast between the soft, almost 'pop,' look of the group and the music, and the harder, weirder context of the lyrics," says designer Sven Mastbooms. **CONCEPT:** "When you see a teddy bear like the one on the cover, you feel like hugging it. However, the metallic surface makes it more assertive and weird. That contrast was continued on the inside of the booklet by introducing 3-D graphics such as the milk bottle, the metallic teddy bears and the 1950s industrial or 'happy happy' illustrations. Although they were very pleased with the artwork in the beginning, the record company and the group weren't amused when posters with the metallic teddy bear were stolen by fans within an hour after they were distributed in clubs and record stores."

AS WE DROVE BACK
TO CAMP, BEN AND I
HAD THE FOLLOWING
CONVERSATION:
Boy, I sure love my
new flashlight.
You know
how much?
No. How much?
I love it so much,
I'm going to take it up
to heaven when I go.
Well, they say you can't take it with you, but I'm not sure they were
talking about flashlights.
Tell you what – I'll
go up first, then
you can come up
after me.
Well...it could happen that way. Sure.
You would have to
come up, because
you would have a
broken heart.
Yes. Yes, I would.

STUDIO: GibbsBaronet, Dallas, TX **ART DIRECTORS:** Steve Gibbs, Willie Baronet **DESIGNER:** Meta Newhouse **PHOTOGRAPHER:** Andy Post **CLIENT/SERVICE:** Andy Post/photography **SOFTWARE:** QuarkXPress **PAPER:** Fox River Confetti, French Construction, French Dur-o-Tone, Potlatch Quintessence **COLORS:** 4, process plus varnish (a second run was produced in black only) **PAGES:** 40 **SIZE:** 7 ¾" x 5" (19.7cm x 12.8cm) **PRINT RUN:** 3,000 **TYPEFACES:** Gill Sans, Garamond **INSPIRATION:** "The story, of course," says designer Meta Newhouse. A father and son going camping discuss whether the father's heart would break if the son died. "It was so heartwarming (and true) that it was important for the design not to get in the way of the storytelling." **CONCEPT:** "The photographer wanted to share a very personal story as a way to present his work. We used Garamond to speak for Ben (the little boy) and Gill Sans for the dad; type size and scale were manipulated to reflect the speaker's mood. Photography was cropped into progressive squares to help give a sense of time passing. We wanted the piece to feel like a keepsake, so we had Andy's kids make leaf rubbings and paste in real leaves (as if from a camping trip). A select few prospective clients were mailed the piece in old cigar boxes with found objects like marbles, matchbooks and pieces of metal, so that they would feel like they were discovering something old, treasured, special." **SPECIAL PRODUCTION TECHNIQUES:** "The four-color pages were printed using dryography, a 300-line waterless printing process. The leaf rubbings, rubberbanding, etc., were all done by hand." **SPECIAL COST-CUTTING TECHNIQUES:** "Two small print runs, one with four-color process and one with just one color. The addition of colored (but unprinted) pages added depth to the brochure at little cost."

STUDIO: Cahan & Associates, San Francisco, CA **ART DIRECTOR:** Bill Cahan **DESIGNER:** Bob Dinetz **ILLUSTRATOR:** Bob Dinetz **PHOTOGRAPHERS:** Unknown (family portraits) **CLIENT/PRODUCT:** Geron Corp./biopharmaceuticals **SOFTWARE:** QuarkXPress **PAPER:** Potlatch Makers' Matte **PAGES:** 56 plus cover **SIZE:** 10½" x 8½" (26.7cm x 21.6cm) **TYPEFACES:** Trixie, Times, Courier **CONCEPT:** "While presenting Geron's science in an understandable format was a basic need," says designer Bob Dinetz, "the intent was to highlight the inescapable process of aging and how it affects the quality of our lives as we grow older. Geron also wanted to feature some of its employees and convey how disease in their own families gives their work a personal perspective. To support this theme, life stories, company milestones and science platforms are depicted in a handmade, intimate manner. The result is a message that disease is not fair or predictable, and that as we live our lives and grow older, we are all vulnerable."

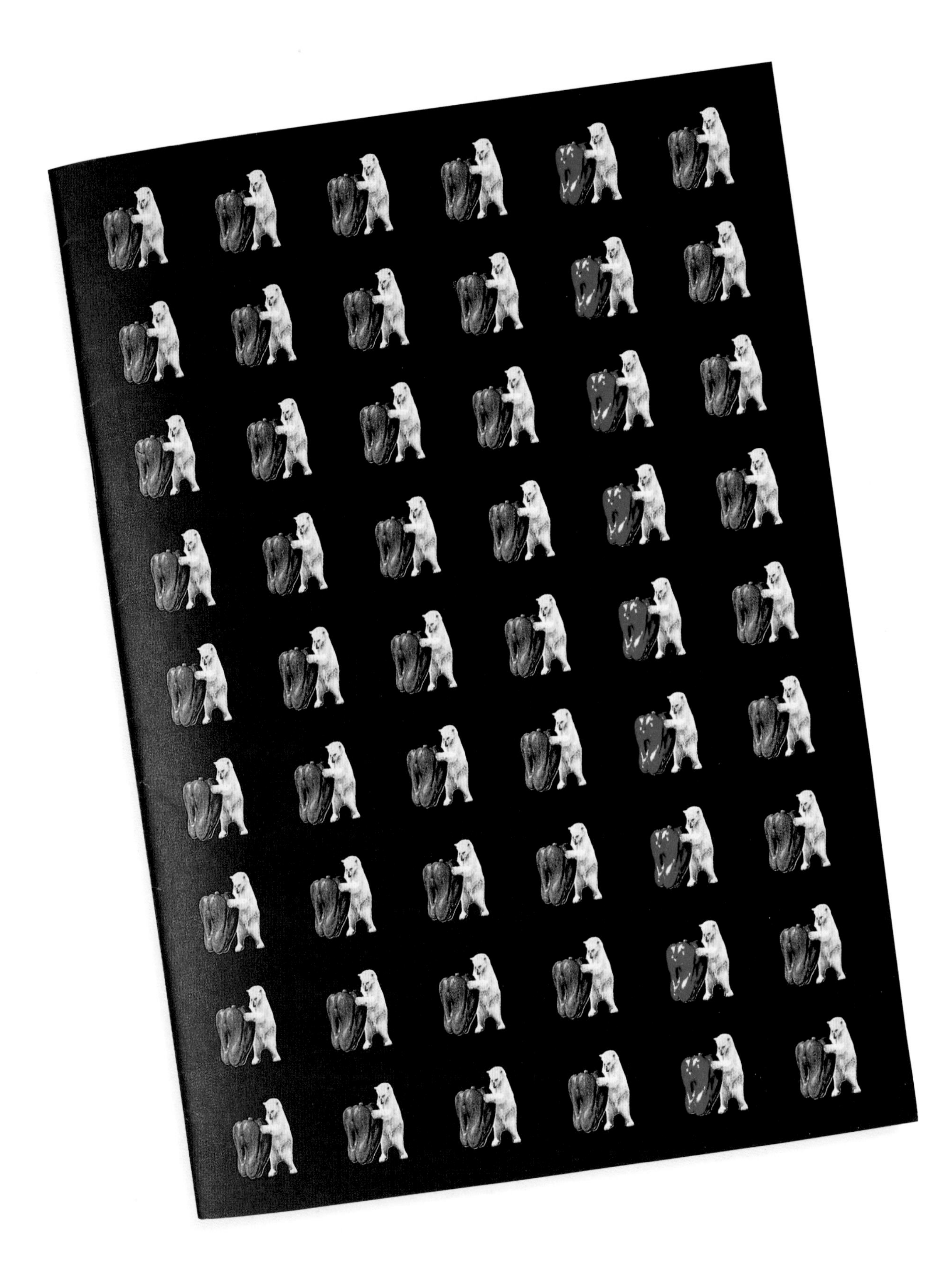

STUDIO: Osoxile S.L., Barcelona, Spain **ART DIRECTOR:** Carmelo Hernando **DESIGNER:** Isabel Barber **PHOTOGRAPHER:** Antonio Ferro **CLIENT/PRODUCT:** Self/design and cultural merchandising **SOFTWARE:** Adobe Photoshop, QuarkXPress **PAGES:** 32 **SIZE:** 8¼" x 5⅞" (21cm x 14.8cm) **COST PER UNIT:** 995 ptas. (English, digital printing); 115 ptas. (Spanish, offset) **TYPEFACES:** Gill Sans, Palatino, Avenir, Futura **CONCEPT:** Osoxile makes the type of objects sold in museum stores: lamps depicting ancient friezes, wooden boxes reproducing medieval originals. It also creates original graphic design and three-dimensional objects for private clients. This catalog, a limited-edition English-language version of the Spanish catalog, was digitally printed.

The British Museum™ © The Trustees of the British Museum 1999 licensed by Copyri
British Museum Soap
150 gr.
Natural Soap 100%. Composition: Sodium cocoate, Aqua, Lauryl Alcohol, Sucrose, Glycerine, Sodium Chloride, Parfum, Pentasodium Pentetate
References
00110 A / Theban
00110 B / Rings
00110 C / Lohan
00110 E / Fig
00110 F / Medlar
A
B
C
D
E
F
A Painted and modelled wooden mummy board of a Theban priestess. Late
Dynasty, about 950 BC.
mask showing the deceased richly adorned
uding a number of real finger-rings.
belonging to a series of Lohans in the
are portraits of individual monks. The
can be seen in the brilliant glazes.
ent group. Ming Dynasty, 16th century AD.
Buddhism. From the late Tang dynasty such
mmon.
entitled Fig and Medlar respectively, we
Morgues (c. 1533-1588), under the patrona
© Osoxile 1999
The Mallorcan Turkey
Papier mâché and bamboo, hand painted
Height 220 mm., base 150 × 125 mm.
Text in Spanish, English, French and German
El Pavo de Mallorca
papier mâché and painted by hand, is one of the Mallorcan
a great deal of admiration and which
Reference 00610 / Turkey
© Osoxile 1999
Just Live Here
Exadure, thyme, lead, moss and artificial grass. Hand painted
100 × 72 × 35 mm.

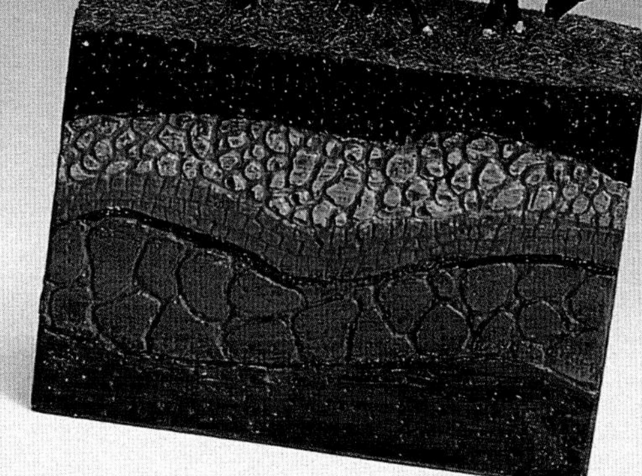

Reference 00510 / Bull

Those moonstruck bulls, the same bulls that carried off the old Europe, later suffered the revenge of their victim, who hunted them from their natural habitat in the name of civilisation and progress.

They found their ecological niche in Spain, and here they have remained, grazing in the meadows, until they meet their death in the summer *at five in the afternoon...*

This piece of Spanish soil is a souvenir or memento for the tourists who come to visit us and also, why not, for our own collection of useless but beautiful fetishes.

A different way of thinking of the country of *Bullfighting* and another look at the reality that, although it is almost a cliché in its anthropological version, it is often ignored in its eco-biological dimension.

This is the implicit contradiction that is the real existence of this beautiful and powerful animal called Toro Bravo.

For him, *Eros* and *Tanatos*, and for his sustained continuity thanks to *Show Business* we raise our glasses and drink a toast to the future, for another three thousand years at least.

Note: In the evergreen oak there would have been bee-eaters and on its back insect-eating-birds if the scale had permitted.

STUDIO: Pentagram Design, New York, NY **ART DIRECTOR:** Paula Scher **DESIGNERS:** Paula Scher, Anke Stohlmann, Keith Daigle **WRITER:** Paula Scher **PRODUCTION MANAGER:** The Actualizers **ILLUSTRATOR:** Pentagram "Iconomics," Issue 2 **PHOTOGRAPHERS:** Richard Bachmann, Classic Stock, Image Bank, Jay Maisel, Panoramic Images, PhotoDisc, Stockbyte, Tony Stone, Vintage Superstock **CLIENT:** Mohawk Paper Mills, Inc. **SOFTWARE:** Adobe Photoshop, Adobe Illustrator, QuarkXPress **PAPER:** Mohawk Superfine **COLORS:** 4, process plus 2, match and varnishes **PAGES:** 14 **SIZE:** 11" x 11¼" (27.9cm x 28.6cm) **PRINT RUN:** 50,000 **TYPEFACES:** Franklin Gothic, various **CONCEPT:** "This piece is designed like the usual paper promotion, demonstrating all of Mohawk Superfine's potential design uses on various weights and shades," says Pentagram. "In spirit, however, the piece is more subversive. It pokes fun at the fact that we, as designers, take ourselves too seriously. With computers, any design, no matter how cutting-edge, is easily cannibalized. 'Your Name Here' gives you the option to do it without even feeling guilty or ashamed. It tells you to steal its design. It's a cheat sheet for designers. The piece also demonstrates that the paper is terrific for a wide range of stuff. In the past, Superfine has been popular for books; this piece shows it's good for anything from stationery to posters to book jackets to product catalogs, and for laser printing." **SPECIAL PRODUCTION TECHNIQUES:** "All images are 175-line screen. Overall matte aqueous coating was used for protection on the front and back cover, book jacket front, poster front, hangtag front, and the outside of the catalog. Spot matte varnish was used for protection throughout the annual report. The announcement card was printed on a full digital image press, the Heidelberg Quickmaster DI."

STUDIO: Inox Design, Milan, Italy **ART DIRECTORS:** Mauro Pastore, Sabrina Elena **DESIGNERS:** Claudio Gavazzi, Renzo Pergher **CLIENT:** MTV Networks **SOFTWARE:** QuarkXPress, Adobe Illustrator **COLORS:** 1, screen-printing (plastic cover); 4, process (brochure) **PAGES:** 32 **SIZE:** 8 ¼" x 4 ¾" (21.1cm x 12cm) **PRINT RUN:** 4,000 with plastic cover, 12,000 without **TYPEFACES:** Kennel District, Murray Hill, Decorated, Spumoni **CONCEPT:** One quarter of the print run was bolted to a screen-printed, pink acrylic sheet. The rest have a die-cut cover. The 1970s-inspired design features bright colors and a female cartoon character. Throughout the piece, pictures of the nominated bands run next to sponsor advertisements, both sharing the same "hip" design sensibility. Brochures were mailed in bright yellow corrugated paper envelopes.

STUDIO: Polka design, Roermond, The Netherlands **GRAPHIC DESIGN:** Joep Pohlen **TEXT:** Joep Pohlen **PHOTOGRAPHERS:** Peter Wijnands, Joep Pohlen **CLIENTS:** Valkenburg Printers Echt, Self **SOFTWARE:** QuarkXPress, Adobe Photoshop **PAPER:** Canson Satin, Gmund Kaschmir black, Bioset, Gill Clear Oxford **COLORS:** 4, process **PAGES:** 34 **SIZE:** 6¼" x 8⅝" (16cm x 22cm) (booklet); 6½" x 9⅛" (16.5cm x 23.2cm) (box) **TYPEFACE:** FF StampGothic (Just van Rossum) **CONCEPT:** "Every year, Valkenburg Printers and Polka design produce a New Year's gift for customers and relatives," explains designer Joep Pohlen. "The subject is always a social issue that was a hot item in the past year. This booklet deals with the problems of the refugees everywhere in the world and how they feel. Peter Wijnands, a news photographer, provided pictures from Bosnia and Afghanistan. A little story on the right-hand pages tells about my family holiday at the Côte d'Azur in France, when we had to flee because of a forest fire. At that moment, we realized how it was to leave everything behind—the toys the children loved, clothes, shoes, a simple comb, a piece of soap. Happily, we got food and a place to sleep from French people who tried to help any way they could. This story, which could happen to almost everyone, tries to help the reader understand the feelings of refugees: They don't choose to be away from their homes. The booklet ends with best wishes for the New Year to our customers and relatives, and also to refugees who want to feel at home somewhere." **SPECIAL FEATURES:** Specially die-cut pages hold two color postcards. The booklet is spiral-bound into a die-cut box that unfolds and becomes a case.

[concept]

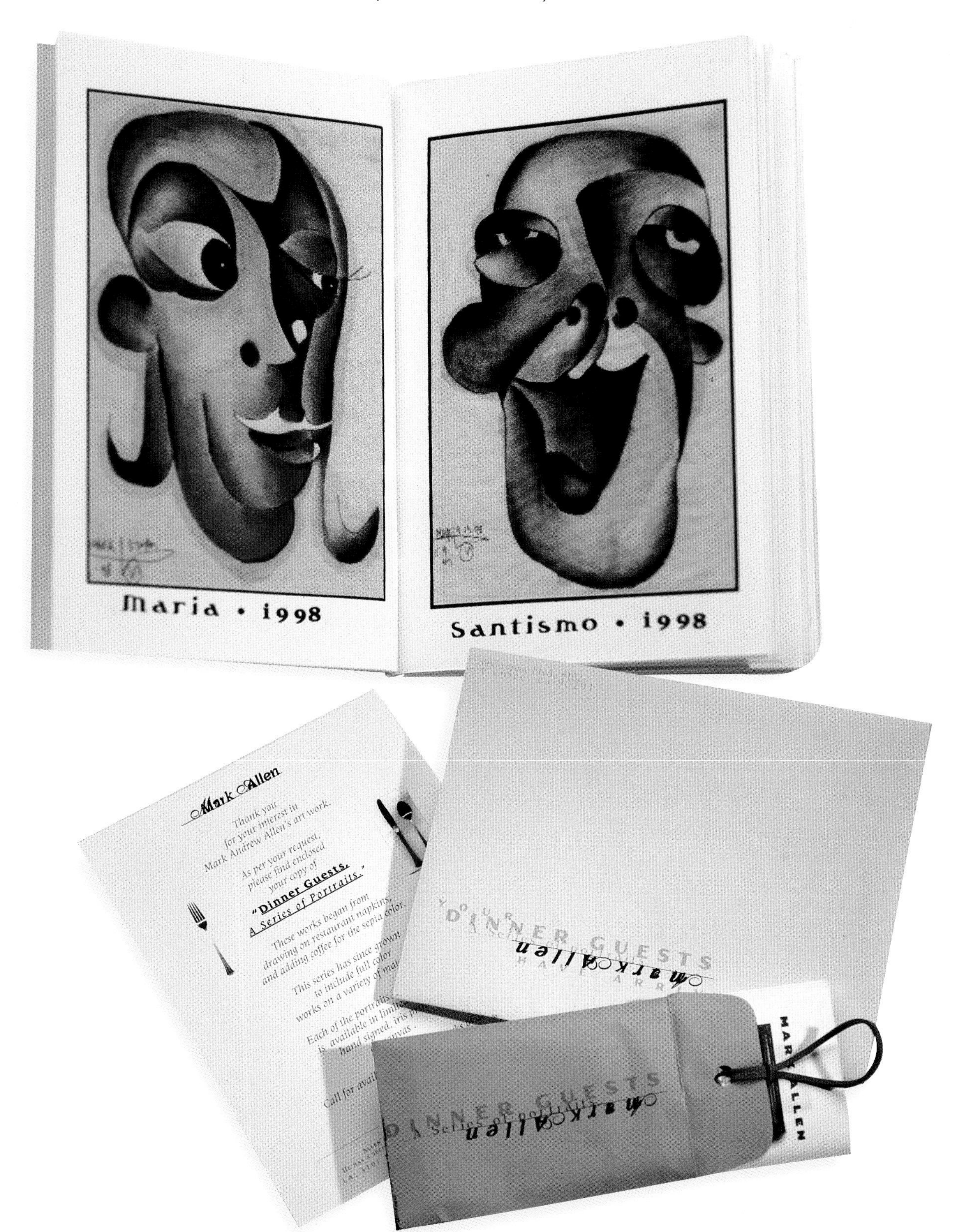

STUDIO: Mark Allen Design, Venice, CA **ART DIRECTOR:** Mark Allen **DESIGNER:** Mark Allen **ARTIST:** Mark Allen **CLIENT:** Self **SOFTWARE:** Adobe Photoshop, QuarkXPress **PAPER:** Great White Inkjet two-sided paper **COLORS:** 4, process **PAGES:** 48 **SIZE:** 2 ¾" x 2" (5cm x 7cm) (booklet) **PRINT RUN:** 200 and counting... **COST PER UNIT:** approx. US$1.42 **TYPEFACES:** Meridien, Template Gothic, Dogma, Fandango **INSPIRATION:** "You ever notice when people ask, 'Oh, you are an artist, huh? What kind of crappy art do you do?' The answer is always the same: 'Well...it's, uh...you really got to see it. I'm doing this thing with color and....It's really hard to explain with words. You really just got see it.' Something like that usually transpires," says artist Mark Allen. "Amazing to me, that we forget sometimes what we are really doing. Here we are visual communicators, yet we seem to fall stupid when it comes to communicating what we are doing to the audience we seek. I thought, hmm, why not have some way cool book small enough to fit in my pocket I could produce at just the right moment when someone asks, 'What kind of crappy art do you do?' and that shows exactly what I do." **CONCEPT:** "I wanted to make a book small enough that it would be very affordable to print and that I could carry several books in my pocket when I go out and about. Sort of like a 48-page business card that showcases some of my new work." **SPECIAL PRODUCTION TECHNIQUES:** "Coffee." **SPECIAL FOLDS OR FEATURES:** "Hand-folded, cut, stapled, crammed into tiny envelopes (printed in-house), and bound with a rubber band."

GESCHAFFEN, UM ANDEREN
DEN RANG ABZULAUFEN.
EINE TIEFE
FREUNDSCHAFT
BEGINNT.
YOU KNOW?
DIE IHR
ERSCHEINUNGSBILD
VON GRUND AUF
PFLEGEN.
YOU KNOW
SHOES
DIE SIE MORGENS
NICHT SCHON ZWEIFELN
LASSEN, OB SIE TAGS-
ÜBER GUT AUSSEHEN.

STUDIO: HEBE Werbung & Design, Leonberg, Germany **ART DIRECTOR:** Reiner Hebe **DESIGNER:** Achim Petroschka **PHOTOGRAPHER:** Stefanos Notopoulos **CLIENT/PRODUCT:** NORD-WEST-RING EG/shoes **SOFTWARE:** QuarkXPress **COLORS:** 4, match **PAGES:** 28 **SIZE:** 11¹¹⁄₁₆" x 8³⁄₈" (29.7cm x 21.3cm) **TYPEFACE:** Franklin Gothic Extra Condensed **INSPIRATION:** "A new view of a new product," say the designers.

Wall
Wax
Toilet
Term

Gold
Cat
Monk
Blow

STUDIO: Cahan & Associates, San Francisco, CA **ART DIRECTOR:** Bill Cahan **DESIGNERS:** Bob Dinetz, Kevin Roberson **ILLUSTRATOR:** Riccardo Vecchio **PHOTOGRAPHERS:** Bob Dinetz, Kevin Roberson **CLIENT:** Mohawk Paper Mills **SOFTWARE:** QuarkXPress **PAPER:** Mohawk Options **PAGES:** 64 plus cover **SIZE:** 10 ½" x 8 ¼" (26.8cm x 21cm) **TYPEFACE:** Avenir **CONCEPT:** Ambiguous and mysterious, the book uses photographs, words, illustrations and even CMYK color samples to explore the idea of "options." **SPECIAL PRODUCTION TECHNIQUES:** On the cover, the title is embossed. Various combinations of colors and varnish are used throughout.

Ladle Rat Rotten Hut

A story to read out loud by H. L. Chace

STUDIO: Pentagram Design, New York, NY **ART DIRECTOR:** Michael Bierut **DESIGNERS:** Michael Bierut, Jennifer Blum **WRITER:** H.L. Chace **PRINTER:** The Stinehour Press **CLIENT:** Self **SOFTWARE:** Adobe Illustrator, QuarkXPress **PAGES:** 14 **SIZE:** 5¾" x 4⅛" (14.8cm x 10.5cm) **TYPEFACE:** Century Schoolbook **INSPIRATION:** "The Pentagram partners take turns researching and designing their annual holiday book, which is mailed as a season's greeting to friends and colleagues," says Pentagram. "The books usually contain some kind of game or activity for friends to share at a holiday gathering. The 1998 edition was 'Ladle Rat Rotten Hut,' a phonetic translation of the story 'Little Red Riding Hood,' created more than 50 years ago by a language professor to demonstrate the importance of intonation." **CONCEPT:** "I first heard 'Ladle Rat Rotten Hut' as a recitation—a girl I was with in college knew it by heart," says designer Michael Bierut. "I think I ran into the occasional reference since then. When I thought it might be a good Pentagram holiday card, I tracked it down on the trusty Internet. The illustration are archival engravings. In keeping with the children's book approach, we used Century Schoolbook exclusively as the typeface. Stinehour Press used letterpress for the black plate and offset for the solid colors. The people that love it really love it. The others don't even get it at all. I do a pretty good reading, but not as good as my friend in college." **SPECIAL PRODUCTION TECHNIQUE:** Letterpress.

[concept]

Wan moaning, Rat Rotten Hut's murder colder inset: "Ladle Rat Rotten Hut, heresy ladle basking winsome burden barter an shirker cockles. Tick disc ladle basking tudor cordage offer groin murder hoe lifts honor udder site offer florist. Shaker lake, dun stopper laundry wrote, end yonder nor sorghum stenc[illegible] stopper torc[illegible]"

attar cordage an ranker dough ball. "Comb ink, sweat hard," setter wicket woof, disgracing is verse. Ladle Rat Rotten Hut entity bet rum end stud buyer groin murder's bet.

"Oh grammar," crater ladle gull, "Wart bag icer gut! A nervous sausage bag ice!" "Butter lucky chew whiff, doling," whiskered disc ratchet woof, wetter wicket small.

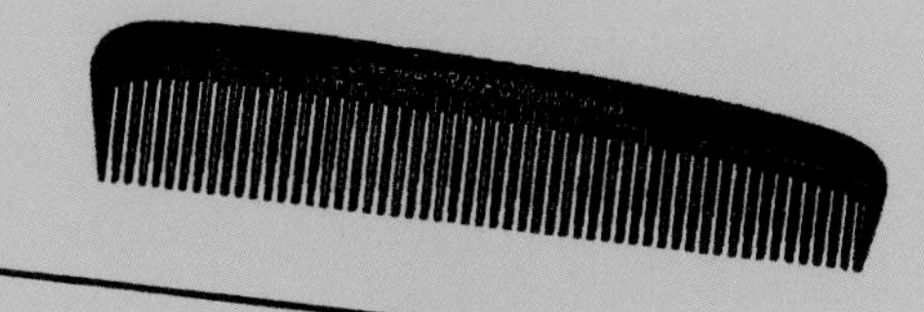

INDEX OF DESIGN FIRMS

INDEX OF PROJECTS

COPYRIGHT NOTICES

- P.10 © Creative Activity Design Company, 1999
- P.11 © 1996 by Peep Show
- Pp. 12–13 Catalogue design and art direction ©1998 The Designers Republic Ltd.
- P.14 © Southern Methodist University, 1998
- P.15 © Pentagram Design
- P.16 © Cahan & Associates
- P.17 © 1998 Etec Systems
- P.18 © 1999 Murphy design inc.
- P.19 © Visual Dialogue, 1998
- P.20 © Acrobat. All copyrights are reserved for Acrobat.
- P.21 ©1993 Büro für Gestaltung: Christoph Burkardt, Albrecht Hotz
- Pp. 22–23 © Brainstorm, Inc., 1998
- P.24 © HEBE Werbung & Design
- P.25 © Adams Outdoor Advertising 1998
- P.26 © Jennifer Sterling Design
- P.27 © Jennifer Sterling Design
- P.28 ©1999 Murphy design inc.
- P.29 © Mark Salisbury/Salisbury Photographers
- Pp. 30–31 © Fachhochschule Hannover, Fachbereich Kunst und Design
- P.32 © Mires Design, Inc.
- P.33 © Gee + Chung Design, 1999
- P.34 © Philip Fass, 1998
- P.35 © Michael Gunselman Inc.
- P.36 © Todd Childers Graphic Design, 1999
- P.37 © 1999 Murphy design inc.
- Pp. 38–39 © Prototype 21, 1999

- Pp. 42–43 Photos © Steve Grubman Photography; Design © Liska + Associates, Inc.
- P.44 © Seven Productions
- P.45 © Mires Design, Inc.
- P.46 © Base Art Co., 1999
- P.47 © Nielinger & Rohsiepe Design
- P.48 1998 © Appleton Papers
- P.49 © João Machado Design Lda.
- Pp. 50–51 © 1998 The Designers Republic Ltd.
- P.52 © Eg.G 1998
- P.53 © 1998 Miriello Grafico, Inc.
- P.54 © MIC*ITAYA and Power of Beauty Co., Ltd.
- P.55 © Sibley Peteet Design 1993
- P.56 © 1995 Lai Lee Choo, Ng Eng Teck, Tan Tuan Yong
- P.57 Design © 1998, Storm Visual Communications; Photography © 1998 Headlight Innovative Imagery
- Pp. 58–59 © Diefenbach Elkins Davies Baron
- P.60 © Art Chantry
- P.61 © Ricardo Mealha, Atelier de Design, Lda.

P.62 © 1998 Cadmus Communications. All rights reserved.
P.63 ©1998 Identix Inc.
P.64 © Louey/Rubino Design Group, Inc. 1998
P.65 © 1999 Plazm Media, Inc.
Pp.66–67 © MIC*ITAYA and Power of Beauty Co., Ltd.
P.68 © Weaver Design 1997
P.69 © Racine Photo Arts, 1998
P.70 © Ricardo Mealha, Atelier de Design, Lda.
P.71 © Ricardo Mealha, Atelier de Design, Lda.
P.72 © Mark Allen Design, 1999
P.73 © VMGD and Sabine Kussmaul, 1998

P.76 © Ricardo Mealha, Atelier de Design, Lda.
P.77 © Curium Design, 1997
P.78 © Eg.G, 1998
P.79 © 1998 Infinite Studio
Pp.80–81 © RTS Rieger Team
Pp.82–83 © American Institute of Graphic Arts, 1997
P.84 © VWA Group, Inc.
P.85 © 1998, Stanley Theatre Society
P.86 © 1996 Watson Wyatt Worldwide
P.87 © CE Software Inc., 1995
P.88 © AL Dermenghem
P.89 © 1998 Apco Worldwide
Pp.90–91 © Dupla Design
P.92 All Rights Reserved © Michel Tcherevkoff
P.93 © Visual Asylum
P.94 © Design Narrative
P.95 © Dupla Design
Pp.96–97 © Dupla Design

P.100 © Mires Design, Inc.
P.101 © Brainstorm, Inc., 1999
P.102 © 1998, Cellotape, Inc.
P.103 © Art Chantry and Jamie Sheehan
P.104 © Big Eye Creative Inc., 1998
P.105 © Big Eye Creative Inc., 1998
Pp.106–107 © Dickson's Inc./Williamson Printing Corp.
P.108 © Visual Dialogue, 1998
P.109 © Visual Dialogue, 1998
P.110 © After Hours Creative
P.111 © Mohawk Paper Mills, Inc. May, 1997
P.112 © Executive Arts Inc.
P.113 © 1998, Stojan
P.114 © Inox Design, 1998
P.115 © Sibley Peteet Design, 1994
Pp.116–117 © Visual Asylum

P.118 © 1998, John Brady Design Consultants Inc.
P.119 © 1997, John Brady Design Consultants Inc.
P.120 © Design Guys 1997
P.121 © Kan & Lau Design Consultants
P.122 © Mindconcept Design
P.123 © MASS MoCA 1998. All rights reserved.
P.124 © Visual Asylum
P.125 © Visual Asylum

P.128 © 1999, CookSherman
P.129 © [i]e design
P.130 © Amy Fowler
P.131 © 5D Studio, 1998
P.132 © Richard Hollant 1998
P.133 © Cahan & Associates
P.134 © Base Art Co., 1999
P.135 © Pat Taylor Inc.
Pp.136–137 © 1998 Fierce Leather
P.138 © 1998 Cadmus Communications. All rights reserved.
P.139 © Cahan & Associates
P.140 © CFD Design 1999
P.141 © Seven Productions
P.142 © GibbsBaronet, 1997
P.143 © Cahan & Associates
Pp.144–145 © Osoxile S.L., 1999
P.146 © Pentagram Design
P.147 © Inox Design, 1998
P.148 © Polka design
P.149 © Mark Allen Design, 1999
P.150 © HEBE Werbung & Design
P.151 © Cahan & Associates
Pp.152–153 © Pentagram Design

008047

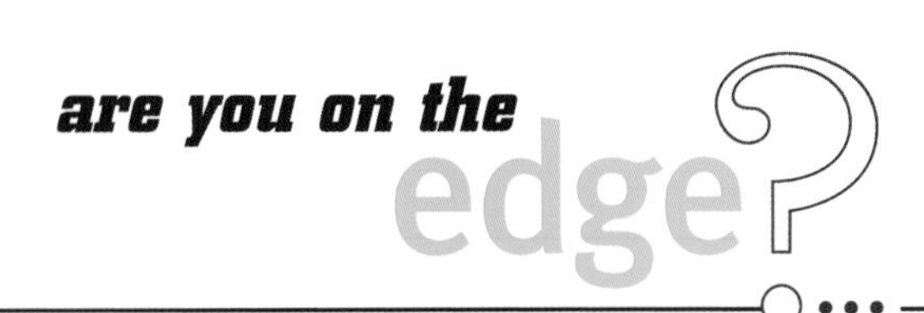

If you'd like for your work to be considered for the next Creative Edge book, please copy the form below (or include the same information in a note to us) and send it to:

LINDA HWANG
Creative Edge mailing list
North Light Books
1507 Dana Avenue
Cincinnati, OH 45207

or call Linda at (513) 531-2222, fax her at (513) 531-4744, or E-mail her (lindah@fwpubs.com). Who knows—maybe you've got the edge we're looking for.

PLEASE PUT ME ON YOUR MAILING LIST TO RECEIVE CALLS FOR ENTRIES FOR FUTURE CREATIVE EDGE BOOKS.

My name

Studio name

Address

City

State Zip Code

Country

Phone

Fax

E-mail

DATE DUE

43395010030984427726012

CHARTERHOUSE LIBRARY
008047